I0439209

Alaska Days with John Muir, by Samual Hall

Title: Alaska Days with John Muir

Author: Samual Hall Young

Release Date: December 17, 2009 [eBook #30697]

Language: English

Character set encoding: ISO-8859-1

START OF THE PROJECT GUTENBERG EBOOK ALASKA DAYS WITH JOHN MUIR

E-text prepared by Greg Bergquist, Chris Curnow, and the Project Gutenberg Online Distributed Proofreading Team (http://www.pgdp.net) from digital material generously made available by Internet Archive/Canadian Libraries (http://www.archive.org/details/toronto)

Note: Project Gutenberg also has an HTML version of this file which includes the original illustrations. See 30697-h.htm or 30697-h.zip:
(http://www.gutenberg.org/files/30697/30697-h/30697-h.htm) or
(http://www.gutenberg.org/files/30697/30697-h.zip)

Images of the original pages are available through Internet Archive/Canadian Libraries. See
http://www.archive.org/details/alaskadayswithjo00younuoft

ALASKA DAYS WITH JOHN MUIR

[Illustration: JOHN MUIR WITH ALASKA SPRUCE CONES]

ALASKA DAYS WITH JOHN MUIR

by

S. HALL YOUNG

Illustrated

[Illustration]

New York Chicago Toronto Fleming H. Revell Company London and Edinburgh

New York: 158 Fifth Avenue Chicago: 125 N. Wabash Ave. Toronto: 25 Richmond St., W. London: 21 Paternoster Square Edinburgh: 100 Princes Street

CONTENTS

ILLUSTRATIONS

FACING PAGE

THE MOUNTAIN

THUNDER BAY

Deep calm from God enfolds the land; Light on the mountain top I stand; How peaceful all, but ah, how grand!

Low lies the bay beneath my feet; The bergs sail out, a white-winged fleet, To where the sky and ocean meet.

Their glacier mother sleeps between Her granite walls. The mountains lean Above her, trailing skirts of green.

Each ancient brow is raised to heaven: The snow streams always, tempest-driven, Like hoary locks, o'er chasms riven

By throes of Earth. But, still as sleep, No storm disturbs the quiet deep Where mirrored forms their silence keep.

A heaven of light beneath the sea! A dream of worlds from shadow free! A pictured, bright eternity!

The azure domes above, below (A crystal casket), hold and show, As precious jewels, gems of snow,

Dark emerald islets, amethyst Of far horizon, pearls of mist In pendant clouds, clear icebergs, kissed

By wavelets,--sparkling diamonds rare Quick flashing through the ambient air. A ring of mountains, graven fair

In lines of grace, encircles all, Save where the purple splendors fall On sky and ocean's bridal-hall.

The yellow river, broad and fleet, Winds through its velvet meadows sweet-- A chain of gold for jewels meet.

Pours over all the sun's broad ray; Power, beauty, peace, in one array! My God, I thank Thee for this day.

I

THE MOUNTAIN

In the summer of 1879 I was stationed at Fort Wrangell in southeastern Alaska, whence I had come the year before, a green young student fresh from college and seminary--very green and very fresh--to do what I could towards establishing the white man's civilization among the Thlinget Indians. I had very many things to learn and many more to unlearn.

Thither came by the monthly mail steamboat in July to aid and counsel me in my work three men of national reputation--Dr. Henry Kendall of New York; Dr. Aaron L. Lindsley of Portland, Oregon, and Dr. Sheldon Jackson of Denver and the West. Their wives accompanied them and they were to spend a month with us.

Standing a little apart from them as the steamboat drew to the dock, his peering blue eyes already eagerly scanning the islands and mountains, was a lean, sinewy man of forty, with waving, reddish-brown hair and beard, and shoulders slightly stooped. He wore a Scotch cap and a long, gray tweed ulster, which I have always since associated with him, and which seemed the same garment, unsoiled and unchanged, that he wore later on his northern trips. He was introduced as Professor Muir, the Naturalist. A hearty grip of the hand, and we seemed to coalesce at once in a friendship which, to me at least, has been one of the very best things I have known in a life full of blessings. From the first he was the strongest and most attractive of these four fine personalities to me, and I began to recognize him as my Master who was to lead me into enchanting regions of beauty and mystery, which without his aid must forever have remained unseen by the eyes of my soul. I sat at his feet; and at the feet of his spirit I still sit, a student, absorbed, surrendered, as this "priest of Nature's inmost shrine" unfolds to me the secrets of his "mountains of God."

[Illustration: FORT WRANGELL

Near the mouth of the Stickeen--the starting point of the expeditions]

Minor excursions culminated in the chartering of the little
steamer *Cassiar*, on which our party, augmented by two or three
friends, steamed between the tremendous glaciers and through
the columned canyons of the swift Stickeen River through the
narrow strip of Alaska's cup-handle to Glenora, in British
Columbia, one hundred and fifty miles from the river's mouth.
Our captain was Nat. Lane, a grandson of the famous Senator
Joseph Lane of Oregon. Stocky, broad-shouldered, muscular,
given somewhat to strange oaths and strong liquids, and eying
askance our group as we struck the bargain, he was withal a
genial, good-natured man, and a splendid river pilot.

Dropping down from Telegraph Creek (so named because it was
a principal station of the great projected trans-American and
trans-Siberian line of the Western Union, that bubble pricked by
Cyrus Field's cable), we tied up at Glenora about noon of a
cloudless day.

"Amuse yourselves," said Captain Lane at lunch. "Here we stay
till two o'clock to-morrow morning. This gale, blowing from the
sea, makes safe steering through the Canyon impossible, unless
we take the morning's calm."

I saw Muir's eyes light up with a peculiar meaning as he glanced
quickly at me across the table. He knew the leading strings I was
in; how those well-meaning D.D.s and their motherly wives
thought they had a special mission to suppress all my
self-destructive proclivities toward dangerous adventure, and
especially to protect me from "that wild Muir" and his
hare-brained schemes of mountain climbing.

"Where is it?" I asked, as we met behind the pilot house a
moment later.

He pointed to a little group of jagged peaks rising right up from
where we stood--a pulpit in the center of a vast rotunda of

magnificent mountains. "One of the finest viewpoints in the world," he said.

"How far to the highest point?"

"About ten miles."

"How high?"

"Seven or eight thousand feet."

That was enough. I caught the D.D.s with guile. There were Stickeen Indians there catching salmon, and among them Chief Shakes, who our interpreter said was "The youngest but the headest Chief of all." Last night's palaver had whetted the appetites of both sides for more. On the part of the Indians, a talk with these "Great White Chiefs from Washington" offered unlimited possibilities for material favor; and to the good divines the "simple faith and childlike docility" of these children of the forest were a constant delight. And then how well their high-flown compliments and flowery metaphors would sound in article and speech to the wondering East! So I sent Stickeen Johnny, the interpreter, to call the natives to another *hyou wawa* (big talk) and, note-book in hand, the doctors "went gayly to the fray." I set the speeches a-going, and then slipped out to join the impatient Muir.

"Take off your coat," he commanded, "and here's your supper."

Pocketing two hardtacks apiece we were off, keeping in shelter of house and bush till out of sight of the council-house and the flower-picking ladies. Then we broke out. What a matchless climate! What sweet, lung-filling air! Sunshine that had no weakness in it--as if we were springing plants. Our sinews like steel springs, muscles like India rubber, feet soled with iron to grip the rocks. Ten miles? Eight thousand feet? Why, I felt equal to forty miles and the Matterhorn!

"Eh, mon!" said Muir, lapsing into the broad Scotch he was so fond of using when enjoying himself, "ye'll see the sicht o' yer life the day. Ye'll get that'll be o' mair use till ye than a' the gowd o' Cassiar."

From the first, it was a hard climb. Fallen timber at the mountain's foot covered with thick brush swallowed us up and plucked us back. Beyond, on the steeper slopes, grew dwarf evergreens, five or six feet high--the same fir that towers a hundred feet with a diameter of three or four on the river banks, but here stunted by icy mountain winds. The curious blasting of the branches on the side next to the mountain gave them the appearance of long-armed, humpbacked, hairy gnomes, bristling with anger, stretching forbidding arms downwards to bar our passage to their sacred heights. Sometimes an inviting vista through the branches would lure us in, when it would narrow, and at its upper angle we would find a solid phalanx of these grumpy dwarfs. Then we had to attack boldly, scrambling over the obstinate, elastic arms and against the clusters of stiff needles, till we gained the upper side and found another green slope.

Muir led, of course, picking with sure instinct the easiest way. Three hours of steady work brought us suddenly beyond the timber-line, and the real joy of the day began. Nowhere else have I see anything approaching the luxuriance and variety of delicate blossoms shown by these high, mountain pastures of the North. "You scarce could see the grass for flowers." Everything that was marvelous in form, fair in color, or sweet in fragrance seemed to be represented there, from daisies and campanulas to Muir's favorite, the cassiope, with its exquisite little pink-white bells shaped like lilies-of-the-valley and its subtle perfume. Muir at once went wild when we reached this fairyland. From cluster to cluster of flowers he ran, falling on his knees, babbling in unknown tongues, prattling a curious mixture of scientific lingo and baby talk, worshiping his little blue-and-pink goddesses.

"Ah! my blue-eyed darlin', little did I think to see you here. How did you stray away from Shasta?"

"Well, well! Who'd 'a' thought that you'd have left that niche in the Merced mountains to come here!"

"And who might you be, now, with your wonder look? Is it possible that you can be (two Latin polysyllables)? You're lost, my dear; you belong in Tennessee."

"Ah! I thought I'd find you, my homely little sweetheart," and so on unceasingly.

So absorbed was he in this amatory botany that he seemed to forget my existence. While I, as glad as he, tagged along, running up and down with him, asking now and then a question, learning something of plant life, but far more of that spiritual insight into Nature's lore which is granted only to those who love and woo her in her great outdoor palaces. But how I anathematized my short-sighted foolishness for having as a student at old Wooster shirked botany for the "more important" studies of language and metaphysics. For here was a man whose natural science had a thorough technical basis, while the superstructure was built of "lively stones," and was itself a living temple of love!

With all his boyish enthusiasm, Muir was a most painstaking student; and any unsolved question lay upon his mind like a personal grievance until it was settled to his full understanding. One plant after another, with its sand-covered roots, went into his pockets, his handkerchief and the "full" of his shirt, until he was bulbing and sprouting all over, and could carry no more. He was taking them to the boat to analyze and compare at leisure. Then he began to requisition my receptacles. I stood it while he stuffed my pockets, but rebelled when he tried to poke the prickly, scratchy things inside my shirt. I had not yet attained that sublime indifference to physical comfort, that Nirvana of passivity, that Muir had found.

Hours had passed in this entrancing work and we were progressing upwards but slowly. We were on the southeastern slope of the mountain, and the sun was still staring at us from a cloudless sky. Suddenly we were in the shadow as we worked around a spur of rock. Muir looked up, startled. Then he jammed home his last handful of plants, and hastened up to where I stood.

"Man!" he said, "I was forgetting. We'll have to hurry now or we'll miss it, we'll miss it."

"Miss what?" I asked.

"The jewel of the day," he answered; "the sight of the sunset from the top."

Then Muir began to *slide* up that mountain. I had been with mountain climbers before, but never one like him. A deer-lope over the smoother slopes, a sure instinct for the easiest way into a rocky fortress, an instant and unerring attack, a serpent-glide up the steep; eye, hand and foot all connected dynamically; with no appearance of weight to his body--as though he had Stockton's negative gravity machine strapped on his back.

Fifteen years of enthusiastic study among the Sierras had given him the same pre-eminence over the ordinary climber as the Big Horn of the Rockies shows over the Cotswold. It was only by exerting myself to the limit of my strength that I was able to keep near him. His example was at the same time my inspiration and despair. I longed for him to stop and rest, but would not have suggested it for the world. I would at least be game, and furnish no hint as to how tired I was, no matter how chokingly my heart thumped. Muir's spirit was in me, and my "chief end," just then, was to win that peak with him. The impending calamity of being beaten by the sun was not to be contemplated without horror. The loss of a fortune would be as nothing to that!

[Illustration: THE MOUNTAIN

He pointed to a little group of jagged peaks rising right up from where we stood--a pulpit in the center of a vast rotunda of magnificent mountains]

We were now beyond the flower garden of the gods, in a land of rocks and cliffs, with patches of short grass, caribou moss and lichens between. Along a narrowing arm of the mountain, a deep canyon flumed a rushing torrent of icy water from a small glacier on our right. Then came moraine matter, rounded pebbles and boulders, and beyond them the glacier. Once a giant, it is nothing but a baby now, but the ice is still blue and clear, and the crevasses many and deep. And that day it had to be crossed, which was a ticklish task. A misstep or slip might land us at once fairly into the heart of the glacier, there to be preserved in cold storage for the wonderment of future generations. But glaciers were Muir's special pets, his intimate companions, with whom he held sweet communion. Their voices were plain language to his ears, their work, as God's landscape gardeners, of the wisest and best that Nature could offer.

No Swiss guide was ever wiser in the habits of glaciers than Muir, or proved to be a better pilot across their deathly crevasses. Half a mile of careful walking and jumping and we were on the ground again, at the base of the great cliff of metamorphic slate that crowned the summit. Muir's aneroid barometer showed a height of about seven thousand feet, and the wall of rock towered threateningly above us, leaning out in places, a thousand feet or so above the glacier. But the earth-fires that had melted and heaved it, the ice mass that chiseled and shaped it, the wind and rain that corroded and crumbled it, had left plenty of bricks out of that battlement, had covered its face with knobs and horns, had ploughed ledges and cleaved fissures and fastened crags and pinnacles upon it, so that, while its surface was full of man-traps and blind ways, the human spider might still find some hold for his claws.

The shadows were dark upon us, but the lofty, icy peaks of the main range still lay bathed in the golden rays of the setting sun. There was no time to be lost. A quick glance to the right and left, and Muir, who had steered his course wisely across the glacier, attacked the cliff, simply saying, "We must climb cautiously here."

Now came the most wonderful display of his mountain-craft. Had I been alone at the feet of these crags I should have said, "It can't be done," and have turned back down the mountain. But Muir was my "control," as the Spiritists say, and I never thought of doing anything else but following him. He thought he could climb up there and that settled it. He would do what he thought he could. And such climbing! There was never an instant when both feet and hands were not in play, and often elbows, knees, thighs, upper arms, and even chin must grip and hold. Clambering up a steep slope, crawling under an overhanging rock, spreading out like a flying squirrel and edging along an inch-wide projection while fingers clasped knobs above the head, bending about sharp angles, pulling up smooth rock-faces by sheer strength of arm and chinning over the edge, leaping fissures, sliding flat around a dangerous rock-breast, testing crumbly spurs before risking his weight, always going up, up, no hesitation, no pause--that was Muir! My task was the lighter one; he did the head-work, I had but to imitate. The thin fragment of projecting slate that stood the weight of his one hundred and fifty pounds would surely sustain my hundred and thirty. As far as possible I did as he did, took his hand-holds, and stepped in his steps.

But I was handicapped in a way that Muir was ignorant of, and I would not tell him for fear of his veto upon my climbing. My legs were all right--hard and sinewy; my body light and supple, my wind good, my nerves steady (heights did not make me dizzy); but my arms--there lay the trouble. Ten years before I had been fond of breaking colts--till the colts broke me. On successive summers in West Virginia, two colts had fallen with me and dislocated first my left shoulder, then my right. Since that both arms had been out of joint more than once. My left was especially weak. It would not sustain my weight, and I had to favor it constantly. Now and again, as I pulled myself up some difficult reach I could feel the head of the humerus move from its socket.

Muir climbed so fast that his movements were almost like flying, legs and arms moving with perfect precision and unfailing judgment. I must keep close behind him or I would fail to see his points of vantage. But the pace was a killing one for me. As we neared the summit my strength began to fail, my breath to come in gasps, my muscles to twitch. The overwhelming fear of losing sight of my guide, of being left behind and failing to see that sunset, grew upon me, and I hurled myself blindly at every fresh obstacle, determined to keep up. At length we climbed upon a little shelf, a foot or two wide, that corkscrewed to the left. Here we paused a moment to take breath and look around us. We had ascended the cliff some nine hundred and fifty feet from the glacier, and were within forty or fifty feet of the top.

Among the much-prized gifts of this good world one of the very richest was given to me in that hour. It is securely locked in the safe of my memory and nobody can rob me of it--an imperishable treasure. Standing out on the rounded neck of the cliff and facing the southwest, we could see on three sides of us. The view was much the finest of all my experience. We seemed to stand on a high rostrum in the center of the greatest amphitheater in the world. The sky was cloudless, the level sun flooding all the landscape with golden light. From the base of the mountain on which we stood stretched the rolling upland. Striking boldly across our front was the deep valley of the Stickeen, a line of foliage, light green cottonwoods and darker alders, sprinkled with black fir and spruce, through which the river gleamed with a silvery sheen, now spreading wide among its islands, now foaming white through narrow canyons. Beyond, among the undulating hills, was a marvelous array of lakes. There must have been thirty or forty of them, from the pond of an acre to the wide sheet two or three miles across. The strangely elongated and rounded hills had the appearance of giants in bed, wrapped in many-colored blankets, while the lakes were their deep, blue eyes, lashed with dark evergreens, gazing steadfastly heavenward. Look long at these recumbent forms and you will see the heaving of their breasts.

The whole landscape was alert, expectant of glory. Around this great camp of prostrate Cyclops there stood an unbroken semicircle of mighty peaks in solemn grandeur, some hoary-headed, some with locks of brown, but all wearing white glacier collars. The taller peaks seemed almost sharp enough to be the helmets and spears of watchful sentinels. And the colors! Great stretches of crimson fireweed, acres and acres of them, smaller patches of dark blue lupins, and hills of shaded yellow, red, and brown, the many-shaded green of the woods, the amethyst and purple of the far horizon--who can tell it? We did not stand there more than two or three minutes, but the whole wonderful scene is deeply etched on the tablet of my memory, a photogravure never to be effaced.

THE RESCUE

THE MOUNTAIN'S FAITH

At eventide, upon a dreary sea, I watched a mountain rear its hoary head To look with steady gaze in the near heaven. The earth was cold and still. No sound was heard But the dream-voices of the sleeping sea. The mountain drew its gray cloud-mantle close, Like Roman senator, erect and old, Raising aloft an earnest brow and calm, With upward look intent of steadfast faith. The sky was dim; no glory-light shone forth To crown the mountain's faith; which faltered not, But, ever hopeful, waited patiently.

At morn I looked again. Expectance sat Of immanent glory on the mountain's brow. And, in a moment, lo! the glory *came!* An angel's hand rolled back a crimson cloud. Deep, rose-red light of wondrous tone and power-- A crown of matchless splendor--graced its head, Majestic, kingly, pure as Heaven, yet warm With earthward love. A motion, like a heart With rich blood beating, seemed to sway and pulse, With might of ecstasy, the granite peak. A poem grand it was of Love Divine-- An anthem, sweet and strong, of praise to God-- A victory-peal from barren fields of death. Its gaze was heavenward still, but earthward too-- For Love seeks not her own, and joy is full, Only when freest given. The sun shone forth, And now the mountain doffed its ruby crown For one of diamonds. Still the light streamed down; No longer chill and bleak, the morning glowed With warmth and light, and clouds of fiery hue Mantled the crystal glacier's chilly stream, And all the landscape throbbed with sudden joy.

II

THE RESCUE

Muir was the first to awake from his trance. Like Schiller's king in "The Diver," "Nothing could slake his wild thirst of desire."

"The sunset," he cried; "we must have the whole horizon."

Then he started running along the ledge like a mountain goat, working to get around the vertical cliff above us to find an ascent on the other side. He was soon out of sight, although I followed as fast as I could. I heard him shout something, but could not make out his words. I know now he was warning me of a dangerous place. Then I came to a sharp-cut fissure which lay across my path--a gash in the rock, as if one of the Cyclops had struck it with his axe. It sloped very steeply for some twelve feet below, opening on the face of the precipice above the glacier, and was filled to within about four feet of the surface with flat, slaty gravel. It was only four or five feet across, and I could easily have leaped it had I not been so tired. But a rock the size of my head projected from the slippery stream of gravel. In my haste to overtake Muir I did not stop to make sure this stone was part of the cliff, but stepped with springing force upon it to cross the fissure. Instantly the stone melted away beneath my feet, and I shot with it down towards the precipice. With my peril sharp upon me I cried out as I whirled on my face, and struck out both hands to grasp the rock on either side.

Falling forward hard, my hands struck the walls of the chasm, my arms were twisted behind me, and instantly both shoulders were dislocated. With my paralyzed arms flopping helplessly above my head, I slid swiftly down the narrow chasm. Instinctively I flattened down on the sliding gravel, digging my chin and toes into it to check my descent; but not until my feet hung out over the edge of the cliff did I feel that I had stopped. Even then I dared not breathe or stir, so precarious was my hold on that treacherous shale. Every moment I seemed to be slipping inch by inch to the point when all would give way and I would go whirling down to the glacier.

After the first wild moment of panic when I felt myself falling, I do not remember any sense of fear. But I know what it is to have a thousand thoughts flash through the brain in a single instant--an anguished thought of my young wife at Wrangell, with her immanent motherhood; an indignant thought of the insurance companies that refused me policies on my life; a thought of wonder as to what would become of my poor flocks of Indians among the islands; recollections of events far and near in time, important and trivial; but each thought printed upon my memory by the instantaneous photography of deadly peril. I had no hope of escape at all. The gravel was rattling past me and piling up against my head. The jar of a little rock, and all would be over. The situation was too desperate for actual fear. Dull wonder as to how long I would be in the air, and the hope that death would be instant--that was all. Then came the wish that Muir would come before I fell, and take a message to my wife.

[Illustration: ONE OF THE MARVELOUS ARRAY OF LAKES]

Suddenly I heard his voice right above me. "My God!" he cried. Then he added, "Grab that rock, man, just by your right hand."

I gurgled from my throat, not daring to inflate my lungs, "My arms are out."

There was a pause. Then his voice rang again, cheery, confident, unexcited, "Hold fast; I'm going to get you out of this. I can't get to you on this side; the rock is sheer. I'll have to leave you now and cross the rift high up and come down to you on the other side by which we came. Keep cool."

Then I heard him going away, whistling "The Blue Bells of Scotland," singing snatches of Scotch songs, calling to me, his voice now receding, as the rocks intervened, then sounding louder as he came out on the face of the cliff. But in me hope surged at full tide. I entertained no more thoughts of last messages. I did not see how he could possibly do it, but he was John Muir, and I had seen his wonderful rock-work. So I determined not to fall and made myself as flat and heavy as possible, not daring to twitch a muscle or wink an eyelid, for I still felt myself slipping, slipping down the greasy slate. And now a new peril threatened. A chill ran through me of cold and nervousness, and I slid an inch. I suppressed the growing shivers with all my will. I would keep perfectly quiet till Muir came back. The sickening pain in my shoulders increased till it was torture, and I could not ease it.

It seemed like hours, but it was really only about ten minutes before he got back to me. By that time I hung so far over the edge of the precipice that it seemed impossible that I could last another second. Now I heard Muir's voice, low and steady, close to me, and it seemed a little below.

"Hold steady," he said. "I'll have to swing you out over the cliff."

Then I felt a careful hand on my back, fumbling with the waistband of my pants, my vest and shirt, gathering all in a firm grip. I could see only with one eye and that looked upon but a foot or two of gravel on the other side.

"Now!" he said, and I slid out of the cleft with a rattling shower of stones and gravel. My head swung down, my impotent arms dangling, and I stared straight at the glacier, a thousand feet below. Then my feet came against the cliff.

"Work downwards with your feet."

I obeyed. He drew me close to him by crooking his arm and as my head came up past his level he caught me by my collar with his teeth! My feet struck the little two-inch shelf on which he was standing, and I could see Muir, flattened against the face of the rock and facing it, his right hand stretched up and clasping a little spur, his left holding me with an iron grip, his head bent sideways, as my weight drew it. I felt as alert and cool as he.

"I've got to let go of you," he hissed through his clenched teeth. "I need both hands here. Climb upward with your feet."

How he did it, I know not. The miracle grows as I ponder it. The wall was almost perpendicular and smooth. My weight on his jaws dragged him outwards. And yet, holding me by his teeth as a panther her cub and clinging like a squirrel to a tree, he climbed with me straight up ten or twelve feet, with only the help of my iron-shod feet scrambling on the rock. It was utterly impossible, yet he did it!

When he landed me on the little shelf along which we had come, my nerve gave way and I trembled all over. I sank down exhausted, Muir only less tired, but supporting me.

The sun had set; the air was icy cold and we had no coats. We would soon chill through. Muir's task of rescue had only begun and no time was to be lost. In a minute he was up again, examining my shoulders. The right one had an upward dislocation, the ball of the humerus resting on the process of the scapula, the rim of the cup. I told him how, and he soon snapped the bone into its socket. But the left was a harder proposition. The luxation was downward and forward, and the strong, nervous reaction of the muscles had pulled the head of the bone deep into my armpit. There was no room to work on that narrow ledge. All that could be done was to make a rude sling with one of my suspenders and our handkerchiefs, so as to both support the elbow and keep the arm from swinging.

Then came the task to get down that terrible wall to the glacier, by the only practicable way down the mountain that Muir, after a careful search, could find. Again I am at loss to know how he accomplished it. For an unencumbered man to descend it in the deepening dusk was a most difficult task; but to get a tottery, nerve-shaken, pain-wracked cripple down was a feat of positive wonder. My right arm, though in place, was almost helpless. I could only move my forearm; the muscles of the upper part simply refusing to obey my will. Muir would let himself down to a lower shelf, brace himself, and I would get my right hand against him, crawl my fingers over his shoulder until the arm hung in front of him, and falling against him, would be eased down to his standing ground. Sometimes he would pack me a short distance on his back. Again, taking me by the wrist, he would swing me down to a lower shelf, before descending himself. My right shoulder came out three times that night, and had to be reset.

It was dark when we reached the base; there was no moon and it was very cold. The glacier provided an operating table, and I lay on the ice for an hour while Muir, having slit the sleeve of my shirt to the collar, tugged and twisted at my left arm in a vain attempt to set it. But the ball was too deep in its false socket, and all his pulling only bruised and made it swell. So he had to do up the arm again, and tie it tight to my body. It must have been near midnight when we left the foot of the cliff and started down the mountain. We had ten hard miles to go, and no supper, for the hardtack had disappeared ere we were half-way up the mountain. Muir dared not take me across the glacier in the dark; I was too weak to jump the crevasses. So we skirted it and came, after a mile, to the head of a great slide of gravel, the fine moraine matter of the receding glacier. Muir sat down on the gravel; I sat against him with my feet on either side and my arm over his shoulder. Then he began to hitch and kick, and presently we were sliding at great speed in a cloud of dust. A full half-mile we flew, and were almost buried when we reached the bottom of the slide. It was the easiest part of our trip.

Now we found ourselves in the canyon, down which tumbled the glacial stream, and far beneath the ridge along which we had ascended. The sides of the canyon were sheer cliffs.

"We'll try it," said Muir. "Sometimes these canyons are passable."

But the way grew rougher as we descended. The rapids became falls and we often had to retrace our steps to find a way around them. After we reached the timber-line, some four miles from the summit, the going was still harder, for we had a thicket of alders and willows to fight. Here Muir offered to make a fire and leave me while he went forward for assistance, but I refused. "No," I said, "I'm going to make it to the boat."

All that night this man of steel and lightning worked, never resting a minute, doing the work of three men, helping me along the slopes, easing me down the rocks, pulling me up cliffs, dashing water on me when I grew faint with the pain; and always cheery, full of talk and anecdote, cracking jokes with me, infusing me with his own indomitable spirit. He was eyes, hands, feet, and heart to me--my caretaker, in whom I trusted absolutely. My eyes brim with tears even now when I think of his utter self-abandon as he ministered to my infirmities.

About four o'clock in the morning we came to a fall that we could not compass, sheer a hundred feet or more. So we had to attack the steep walls of the canyon. After a hard struggle we were on the mountain ridges again, traversing the flower pastures, creeping through openings in the brush, scrambling over the dwarf fir, then down through the fallen timber. It was half-past seven o'clock when we descended the last slope and found the path to Glenora. Here we met a straggling party of whites and Indians just starting out to search the mountain for us.

As I was coming wearily up the teetering gang-plank, feeling as if I couldn't keep up another minute, Dr. Kendall stepped upon its end, barring my passage, bent his bushy white brows upon me from his six feet of height, and began to scold:

"See here, young man; give an account of yourself. Do you know you've kept us waiting----"

Just then Captain Lane jumped forward to help me, digging the old Doctor of Divinity with his elbow in the stomach and nearly knocking him off the boat.

"Oh, hell!" he roared. "Can't you see the man's hurt?"

Mrs. Kendall was a very tall, thin, severe-looking old lady, with face lined with grief by the loss of her children. She never smiled. She had not gone to bed at all that night, but walked the deck and would not let her husband or the others sleep. Soon after daylight she began to lash the men with the whip of her tongue for their "cowardice and inhumanity" in not starting at once to search for me.

"Mr. Young is undoubtedly lying mangled at the foot of a cliff, or else one of those terrible bears has wounded him; and you are lolling around here instead of starting to his rescue. For shame!"

When they objected that they did not know where we had gone, she snapped: "Go everywhere until you find him."

Her fierce energy started the men we met. When I came on board she at once took charge and issued her orders, which everybody jumped to obey. She had blankets spread on the floor of the cabin and laid me on them. She obtained some whisky from the captain, some water, porridge and coffee from the steward. She was sitting on the floor with my head in her lap, feeding me coffee with a spoon, when Dr. Kendall came in and began on me again:

"Suppose you had fallen down that precipice, what would your poor wife have done? What would have become of your Indians and your new church?"

Then Mrs. Kendall turned and thrust her spoon like a sword at him. "Henry Kendall," she blazed, "shut right up and leave this room. Have you no sense? Go instantly, I say!" And the good Doctor went.

My recollections of that day are not very clear. The shoulder was in a bad condition--swollen, bruised, very painful. I had to be strengthened with food and rest, and Muir called from his sleep of exhaustion, so that with four other men he could pull and twist that poor arm of mine for an hour. They got it into its socket, but scarcely had Muir got to sleep again before the strong, nervous twitching of the shoulder dislocated it a second time and seemingly placed it in a worse condition than before. Captain Lane was now summoned, and with Muir to direct, they worked for two or three hours. Whisky was poured down my throat to relax my stubborn, pain-convulsed muscles. Then they went at it with two men pulling at the towel knotted about my wrist, two others pulling against them, foot braced to foot, Muir manipulating my shoulder with his sinewy hands, and the stocky Captain, strong and compact as a bear, with his heel against the yarn ball in my armpit, takes me by the elbow and says, "I'll set it or pull the arm off!"

[Illustration: GLACIER--STICKEEN VALLEY

Muir, fresh and enthusiastic as ever, was the pilot of the party across the moraine and upon the great ice mountain]

Well, he almost does the latter. I am conscious of a frightful strain, a spasm of anguish in my side as his heel slips from the ball and kicks in two of my ribs, a snap as the head of the bone slips into the cup--then kindly oblivion.

I was awakened about five o'clock in the afternoon by the return of the whole party from an excursion to the Great Glacier at the Boundary Line. Muir, fresh and enthusiastic as ever, had been the pilot across the moraine and upon the great ice mountain; and I, wrapped like a mummy in linen strips, was able to join in his laughter as he told of the big D.D.'s heroics, when, in the middle of an acre of alder brush, he asked indignantly, in response to the hurry-up calls: "Do you think I'm going to leave my wife in this forest?"

One overpowering regret--one only--abides in my heart as I think back upon that golden day with John Muir. He could, and did, go back to Glenora on the return trip of the *Cassiar*, ascend the mountain again, see the sunset from its top, make charming sketches, stay all night and see the sunrise, filling his cup of joy so full that he could pour out entrancing descriptions for days. While I--well, with entreating arms about one's neck and pleading, tearful eyes looking into one's own, what could one do but promise to climb no more? But my lifelong lamentation over a treasure forever lost, is this: "I never saw the sunset from that peak."

THE VOYAGE

TOW-A-ATT

You are a child, old Friend--a child! As light of heart, as free, as wild; As credulous of fairy tale; As simple in your faith, as frail In reason; jealous, petulant; As crude in manner; ignorant, Yet wise in love; as rough, as mild-- You are a child!

You are a man, old Friend--a man! Ah, sure in richer tide ne'er ran The blood of earth's nobility, Than through your veins; intrepid, free; In counsel, prudent; proud and tall; Of passions full, yet ruling all; No stauncher friend since time began; You are a MAN!

III

THE VOYAGE

The summer and fall of 1879 Muir always referred to as the most interesting period of his adventurous life. From about the tenth of July to the twentieth of November he was in southeastern Alaska. Very little of this time did he spend indoors. Until steamboat navigation of the Stickeen River was closed by the forming ice, he made frequent trips to the Great Glacier--thirty miles up the river, to the Hot Springs, the Mud Glacier and the interior lakes, ranges, forests and flower pastures. Always upon his return (for my house was his home the most of that time) he would be full to intoxication of what he had seen, and dinners would grow cold and lamps burn out while he held us entranced with his impassioned stories. Although his books are all masterpieces of lucid and glowing English, Muir was one of those rare souls who talk better than they write; and he made the trees, the animals, and especially the glaciers, live before us. Somehow a glacier never seemed cold when John Muir was talking about it.

On September nineteenth a little stranger whose expected advent was keeping me at home arrived in the person of our first-born daughter. For two or three weeks preceding and following this event Muir was busy writing his summer notes and finishing his pencil sketches, and also studying the flora of the islands. It was a season of constant rains when the *saanah*, the southeast rain-wind, blew a gale. But these stormy days and nights, which kept ordinary people indoors, always lured him out into the woods or up the mountains.

One wild night, dark as Erebus, the rain dashing in sheets and the wind blowing a hurricane, Muir came from his room into ours about ten o'clock with his long, gray overcoat and his Scotch cap on.

"Where now?" I asked.

"Oh, to the top of the mountain," he replied. "It is a rare chance to study this fine storm."

My expostulations were in vain. He rejected with scorn the proffered lantern: "It would spoil the effect." I retired at my usual time, for I had long since learned not to worry about Muir. At two o'clock in the morning there came a hammering at the front door. I opened it and there stood a group of our Indians, rain-soaked and trembling--Chief Tow-a-att, Moses, Aaron, Matthew, Thomas.

"Why, men," I cried, "what's wrong? What brings you here?"

"We want you play (pray)," answered Matthew.

I brought them into the house, and, putting on my clothes and lighting the lamp, I set about to find out the trouble. It was not easy. They were greatly excited and frightened.

"We scare. All Stickeen scare; plenty cly. We want you play God; plenty play."

By dint of much questioning I gathered at last that the whole tribe were frightened by a mysterious light waving and flickering from the top of the little mountain that overlooked Wrangell; and they wished me to pray to the white man's God and avert dire calamity.

"Some miner has camped there," I ventured.

An eager chorus protested; it was not like the light of a camp-fire in the least; it waved in the air like the wings of a spirit. Besides, there was no gold on the top of a hill like that; and no human being would be so foolish as to camp up there on such a night, when there were plenty of comfortable houses at the foot of the hill. It was a spirit, a malignant spirit.

Suddenly the true explanation flashed into my brain, and I shocked my Indians by bursting into a roar of laughter. In imagination I could see him so plainly--John Muir, wet but happy, feeding his fire with spruce sticks, studying and enjoying the storm! But I explained to my natives, who ever afterwards eyed Muir askance, as a mysterious being whose ways and motives were beyond all conjecture.

"Why does this strange man go into the wet woods and up the mountains on stormy nights?" they asked. "Why does he wander alone on barren peaks or on dangerous ice-mountains? There is no gold up there and he never takes a gun with him or a pick. *Icta mamook*--what make? Why--why?"

The first week in October saw the culmination of plans long and eagerly discussed. Almost the whole of the Alexandrian Archipelago, that great group of eleven hundred wooded islands that forms the southeastern cup-handle of Alaska, was at that time a *terra incognita*. The only seaman's chart of the region in existence was that made by the great English navigator, Vancouver, in 1807. It was a wonderful chart, considering what an absurd little sailing vessel he had in which to explore those intricate waters with their treacherous winds and tides.

But Vancouver's chart was hastily made, after all, in a land of fog and rain and snow. He had not the modern surveyor's instruments, boats or other helps. And, besides, this region was changing more rapidly than, perhaps, any other part of the globe. Volcanic islands were being born out of the depths of the ocean; landslides were filling up channels between the islands; tides and rivers were opening new passages and closing old ones; and, more than all, those mightiest tools of the great Engineer, the glaciers, were furrowing valleys, dumping millions of tons of silt into the sea, forming islands, promontories and isthmuses, and by their recession letting the sea into deep and long fiords, forming great bays, inlets and passages, many of which did not exist in Vancouver's time. In certain localities the living glacier stream was breaking off bergs so fast that the resultant bays were lengthening a mile or more each year. Where Vancouver saw only a great crystal wall across the sea, we were to paddle for days up a long and sinuous fiord; and where he saw one glacier, we were to find a dozen.

My mission in the proposed voyage of discovery was to locate and visit the tribes and villages of Thlingets to the north and west of Wrangell, to take their census, confer with their chiefs and report upon their condition, with a view to establishing schools and churches among them. The most of these tribes had never had a visit from a missionary, and I felt the eager zeal an Eliot or a Martin at the prospect of telling them for the first time the Good News. Muir's mission was to find and study the forests, mountains and glaciers. I also was eager to see these and learn about them, and Muir was glad to study the natives with me--so our plans fitted into each other well.

"We are going to write some history, my boy," Muir would say to me. "Think of the honor! We have been chosen to put some interesting people and some of Nature's grandest scenes on the page of human record and on the map. Hurry! We are daily losing the most important news of all the world."

In many respects we were most congenial companions. We both loved the same poets and could repeat, verse about, many poems of Tennyson, Keats, Shelley and Burns. He took with him a volume of Thoreau, and I one of Emerson, and we enjoyed them together. I had my printed Bible with me, and he had his in his head--the result of a Scotch father's discipline. Our studies supplemented each other and our tastes were similar. We had both lived clean lives and our conversation together was sweet and high, while we both had a sense of humor and a large fund of stories.

But Muir's knowledge of Nature and his insight into her plans and methods were so far beyond mine that, while I was organizer and commander of the expedition, he was my teacher and guide into the inner recesses and meanings of the islands, bays and mountains we explored together.

Our ship for this voyage of discovery, while not so large as Vancouver's, was much more shapely and manageable--a *kladushu etlan* (six fathom) red-cedar canoe. It belonged to our captain, old Chief Tow-a-att, a chief who had lately embraced Christianity with his whole heart--one of the simplest, most faithful, dignified and brave souls I ever knew. He fully expected to meet a martyr's death among his heathen enemies of the northern islands; yet he did not shrink from the voyage on that account.

His crew numbered three. First in importance was Kadishan, also a chief of the Stickeens, chosen because of his powers of oratory, his kinship with Chief Shathitch of the Chilcat tribe, and his friendly relations with other chiefs. He was a born courtier, learned in Indian lore, songs and customs, and able to instruct me in the proper Thlinget etiquette to suit all occasions. The other two were sturdy young men--Stickeen John, our interpreter, and Sitka Charley. They were to act as cooks, camp-makers, oarsmen, hunters and general utility men.

We stowed our baggage, which was not burdensome, in one end of the canoe, taking a simple store of provisions--flour, beans, bacon, sugar, salt and a little dried fruit. We were to depend upon our guns, fishhooks, spears and clamsticks for other diet. As a preliminary to our palaver with the natives we followed the old Hudson Bay custom, then firmly established in the North. We took materials for a *potlatch*,--leaf-tobacco, rice and sugar. Our Indian crew laid in their own stock of provisions, chiefly dried salmon and seal-grease, while our table was to be separate, set out with the white man's viands.

We did not get off without trouble. Kadishan's mother, who looked but little older than himself, strongly objected to my taking her son on so perilous a voyage and so late in the fall, and when her scoldings and entreaties did not avail she said: "If anything happens to my son, I will take your baby as mine in payment."

[Illustration: VOYAGES OF MUIR AND YOUNG 1879 and 1880 IN SOUTHEASTERN ALASKA]

One sunny October day we set our prow to the unknown northwest. Our hearts beat high with anticipation. Every passage between the islands was a corridor leading into a new and more enchanting room of Nature's great gallery. The lapping waves whispered enticing secrets, while the seabirds screaming overhead and the eagles shrilling from the sky promised wonderful adventures.

The voyage naturally divides itself into the human interest and the study of nature; yet the two constantly blended throughout the whole voyage. I can only select a few instances from that trip of six weeks whose every hour was new and strange.

Our captain, taciturn and self-reliant, commanded Muir's admiration from the first. His paddle was sure in the stern, his knowledge of the wind and tide unfailing. Whenever we landed the crew would begin to dispute concerning the best place to make camp. But old Tow-a-att, with the mast in his hand, would march straight as an arrow to the likeliest spot of all, stick down his mast as a tent-pole and begin to set up the tent, the others invariably acquiescing in his decision as the best possible choice.

At our first meal Muir's sense of humor cost us one-third of a roll of butter. We invited our captain to take dinner with us. I got out the bread and other viands, and set the two-pound roll of butter beside the bread and placed both by Tow-a-att. He glanced at the roll of butter and at the three who were to eat, measured with his eye one-third of the roll, cut it off with his hunting knife and began to cut it into squares and eat it with great gusto. I was about to interfere and show him the use we made of butter, but Muir stopped me with a wink. The old chief calmly devoured his third of the roll, and rubbing his stomach with great satisfaction pronounced it "*hyas klosh* (very good) glease."

Of necessity we had chosen the rainiest season of the year in that dampest climate of North America, where there are two hundred and twenty-five rainy days out of the three hundred and sixty-five. During our voyage it did not rain every day, but the periods of sunshine were so rare as to make us hail them with joyous acclamation.

We steered our course due westward for forty miles, then through a sinuous, island-studded passage called Rocky Strait, stopping one day to lay in a supply of venison before sailing on to the village of the Kake Indians. My habit throughout the voyage, when coming to a native town, was to find where the head chief lived, feed him with rice and regale him with tobacco, and then induce him to call all his chiefs and head men together for a council. When they were all assembled I would give small presents of tobacco to each, and then open the floodgate of talk, proclaiming my mission and telling them in simplest terms the Great New Story. Muir would generally follow me, unfolding in turn some of the wonders of God's handiwork and the beauty of clean, pure living; and then in turn, beginning with the head chief, each Indian would make his speech. We were received with joy everywhere, and if there was suspicion at first old Tow-a-att's tearful pleadings and Kadishan's oratory speedily brought about peace and unity.

These palavers often lasted a whole day and far into the night, and usually ended with our being feasted in turn by the chief in whose house we had held the council. I took the census of each village, getting the heads of the families to count their relatives with the aid of beans,--the large brown beans representing men, the large white ones, women, and the small Boston beans, children. In this manner the first census of southeastern Alaska was taken.

Before starting on the voyage, we heard that there was a Harvard graduate, bearing an honored New England name, living among the Kake Indians on Kouyou Island. On arriving at the chief town of that tribe we inquired for the white man and were told that he was camping with the family of a sub-chief at the mouth of a salmon stream. We set off to find him. As we neared the shore we saw a circular group of natives around a fire on the beach, sitting on their heels in the stoical Indian way. We landed and came up to them. Not one of them deigned to rise or show any excitement at our coming. The eight or nine men who formed the group were all dressed in colored four-dollar blankets, with the exception of one, who had on a ragged fragment of a filthy, two-dollar, Hudson Bay blanket. The back of this man was towards us, and after speaking to the chief, Muir and I crossed to the other side of the fire, and saw his face. It was the white man, and the ragged blanket was all the clothing he had upon him! An effort to open conversation with him proved futile. He answered only with grunts and mumbled monosyllables. Thus the most filthy, degraded, hopelessly lost savage that we found in this whole voyage was a college graduate of great New England stock!

"Lift a stone to mountain height and let it fall," said Muir, "and it will sink the deeper into the mud."

At Angoon, one of the towns of the Hootz-noo tribe, occurred an incident of another type. We found this village hilariously drunk. There was a very stringent prohibition law over Alaska at that time, which absolutely forbade the importation of any spirituous liquors into the Territory. But the law was deficient in one vital respect--it did not prohibit the importation of molasses; and a soldier during the military occupancy of the Territory had instructed the natives in the art of making rum. The method was simple. A five-gallon oil can was taken and partly filled with molasses as a base; into that alcohol was placed (if it were obtainable), dried apples, berries, potatoes, flour, anything that would rot and ferment; then, to give it the proper tang, ginger, cayenne pepper and mustard were added. This mixture was then set in a warm place to ferment. Another oil can was cut up into long strips, the solder melted out and used to make a pipe, with two or three turns through cool water,--forming the worm, and the still. Talk about your forty-rod whiskey--I have seen this "hooch," as it was called because these same Hootz-noo natives first made it, kill at more than forty rods, for it generally made the natives *fighting* drunk.

Through the large company of screaming, dancing and singing natives we made our way to the chief's house. By some miracle this majestic-looking savage was sober. Perhaps he felt it incumbent upon him as host not to partake himself of the luxuries with which he regaled his guests. He took us hospitably into his great community house of split cedar planks with carved totem poles for corner posts, and called his young men to take care of our canoe and to bring wood for a fire that he might feast us. The wife of this chief was one of the finest looking Indian women I have ever met,--tall, straight, lithe and dignified. But, crawling about on the floor on all fours, was the most piteous travesty of the human form I have ever seen. It was an idiot boy, sixteen years of age. He had neither the comeliness of a beast nor the intellect of a man. His name was *Hootz-too* (Bear Heart), and indeed all his motions were those of a bear rather than of a human being. Crossing the floor with the swinging gait of a bear, he would crouch back on his haunches and resume his constant occupation of sucking his wrist, into which he had thus formed a livid hole. When disturbed at this horrid task he would strike with the claw-like fingers of the other hand, snarling and grunting. Yet the beautiful chieftainess was his mother, and she *loved* him. For sixteen years she had cared for this monster, feeding him with her choicest food, putting him to sleep always in her arms, taking him with her and guarding him day and night. When, a short time before our visit, the medicine men, accusing him of causing the illness of some of the head men of the village, proclaimed him a witch, and the whole tribe came to take and torture him to death, she fought them like a lioness, not counting her own life dear unto her, and saved her boy.

When I said to her thoughtlessly, "Oh, would you not be relieved at the death of this poor idiot boy?" she saw in my words a threat, and I shall never forget the pathetic, hunted look with which she said:

"Oh, no, it must not be; he shall not die. Is he not my son, *uh-yeet-kutsku* (my dear little son)?"

If our voyage had yielded me nothing but this wonderful instance of mother-love, I should have counted myself richly repaid.

One more human story before I come to Muir's part. It was during the latter half of the voyage, and after our discovery of Glacier Bay. The climax of the trip, so far as the missionary interests were concerned, was our visit to the Chilcat and Chilcoot natives on Lynn Canal, the most northern tribes of the Alexandrian Archipelago. Here reigned the proudest and worst old savage of Alaska, Chief Shathitch. His wealth was very great in Indian treasures, and he was reputed to have cached away in different places several houses full of blankets, guns, boxes of beads, ancient carved pipes, spears, knives and other valued heirlooms. He was said to have stored away over one hundred of the elegant Chilcat blankets woven by hand from the hair of the mountain goat. His tribe was rich and unscrupulous. Its members were the middle-men between the whites and the Indians of the Interior. They did not allow these Indians to come to the coast, but took over the mountains articles purchased from the whites--guns, ammunition, blankets, knives and so forth--and bartered them for furs. It was said that they claimed to be the manufacturers of these wares and so charged for them what prices they pleased. They had these Indians of the Interior in a bondage of fear, and would not allow them to trade directly with the white men. Thus they carried out literally the story told of Hudson Bay traffic,--piling beaver skins to the height of a ten-dollar Hudson Bay musket as the *price* of the musket. They were the most quarrelsome and warlike of the tribes of Alaska, and their villages were full of slaves procured by forays upon the coasts of Vancouver Island, Puget Sound, and as far south as the mouth of the Columbia River. I was eager to visit these large and untaught tribes, and establish a mission among them.

[Illustration: CHILCAT WOMAN WEAVING A BLANKET

Chief Shathitch was said to have over one hundred of the elegant Chilcat blankets, woven by hand, from the hair of the mountain goat]

About the first of November we came in sight of the long, low-built village of Yin-des-tuk-ki. As we paddled up the winding channel of the Chilcat River we saw great excitement in the town. We had hoisted the American flag, as was our custom, and had put on our best apparel for the occasion. When we got within long musket-shot of the village we saw the native men come rushing from their houses with their guns in their hands and mass in front of the largest house upon the beach. Then we were greeted by what seemed rather too warm a reception--a shower of bullets falling unpleasantly around us. Instinctively Muir and I ceased to paddle, but Tow-a-att commanded, "*Ut-ha, ut-ha!*--pull, pull!" and slowly, amid the dropping bullets, we zigzagged our way up the channel towards the village. As we drew near the shore a line of runners extended down the beach to us, keeping within shouting distance of each other. Then came the questions like bullets--"*Gusu-wa-eh?*--Who are you? Whence do you come? What is your business here?" And Stickeen John shouted back the reply:

"A great preacher-chief and a great ice-chief have come to bring you a good message."

The answer was shouted back along the line, and then returned a message of greeting and welcome. We were to be the guests of the chief of Yin-des-tuk-ki, old Don-na-wuk (Silver Eye), so called because he was in the habit of wearing on all state occasions a huge pair of silver-bowed spectacles which a Russian officer had given him. He confessed he could not see through them, but thought they lent dignity to his countenance. We paddled slowly up to the village, and Muir and I, watching with interest, saw the warriors all disappear. As our prow touched the sand, however, here they came, forty or fifty of them, without their guns this time, but charging down upon us with war-cries, "*Hoo-hooh, hoo-hooh*," as if they were going to take us prisoners. Dashing into the water they ranged themselves along each side of the canoe; then lifting up our canoe with us in it they rushed with excited cries up the bank to the chief's house and set us down at his door. It was the Thlinget way of paying us honor as great guests.

Then we were solemnly ushered into the presence of Don-na-wuk. His house was large, covering about fifty by sixty feet of ground. The interior was built in the usual fashion of a chief's house--carved corner posts, a square of gravel in the center of the room for the fire surrounded by great hewn cedar planks set on edge; a platform of some six feet in width running clear around the room; then other planks on edge and a high platform, where the chieftain's household goods were stowed and where the family took their repose. A brisk fire was burning in the middle of the room; and after a short palaver, with gifts of tobacco and rice to the chief, it was announced that he would pay us the distinguished honor of feasting us first.

It was a never-to-be-forgotten banquet. We were seated on the lower platform with our feet towards the fire, and before Muir and me were placed huge washbowls of blue Hudson Bay ware. Before each of our native attendants was placed a great carved wooden trough, holding about as much as the washbowls. We had learned enough Indian etiquette to know that at each course our respective vessels were to be filled full of food, and we were expected to carry off what we could not devour. It was indeed a "feast of fat things." The first course was what, for the Indian, takes the place of bread among the whites,--dried salmon. It was served, a whole washbowlful for each of us, with a dressing of seal-grease. Muir and I adroitly manoeuvred so as to get our salmon and seal-grease served separately; for our stomachs had not been sufficiently trained to endure that rancid grease. This course finished, what was left was dumped into receptacles in our canoe and guarded from the dogs by young men especially appointed for that purpose. Our washbowls were cleansed and the second course brought on. This consisted of the back fat of the deer, great, long hunks of it, served with a gravy of seal-grease. The third course was little Russian potatoes about the size of walnuts, dished out to us, a washbowlful, with a dressing of seal-grease. The final course was the only berry then in season, the long fleshy apple of the wild rose mellowed with frost, served to us in the usual quantity with the invariable sauce of seal-grease.

"Mon, mon!" said Muir aside to me, "I'm fashed we'll be floppin' aboot i' the sea, whiles, wi' flippers an' forked tails."

When we had partaken of as much of this feast of fat things as our civilized stomachs would stand, it was suddenly announced that we were about to receive a visit from the great chief of the Chilcats and the Chilcoots, old Chief Shathitch (Hard-to-Kill). In order to properly receive His Majesty, Muir and I and our two chiefs were each given a whole bale of Hudson Bay blankets for a couch. Shathitch made us wait a long time, doubtless to impress us with his dignity as supreme chief.

The heat of the fire after the wind and cold of the day made us very drowsy. We fought off sleep, however, and at last in came stalking the biggest chief of all Alaska, clothed in his robe of state, which was an elegant chinchilla blanket; and upon its yellow surface, as the chief slowly turned about to show us what was written thereon, we were astonished to see printed in black letters these words, "To Chief Shathitch, from his friend, William H. Seward!" We learned afterwards that Seward, in his voyage of investigation, had penetrated to this far-off town, had been received in royal state by the old chief and on his return to the States had sent back this token of his appreciation of the chief's hospitality. Whether Seward was regaled with viands similar to those offered to us, history does not relate.

To me the inspiring part of that voyage came next day, when I preached from early morning until midnight, only occasionally relieved by Muir and by the responsive speeches of the natives.

"More, more; tell us more," they would cry. "It is a good talk; we never heard this story before." And when I would inquire, "Of what do you wish me now to talk?" they would always say, "Tell us more of the Man from Heaven who died for us."

Runners had been sent to the Chilcoot village on the eastern arm of Lynn Canal, and twenty-five miles up the Chilcat River to Shathitch's town of Klukwan; and as the day wore away the crowd of Indians had increased so greatly that there was no room for them in the large house. I heard a scrambling upon the roof, and looking up I saw a row of black heads around the great smoke-hole in the center of the roof. After a little a ripping, tearing sound came from the sides of the building. They were prying off the planks in order that those outside might hear.

When my voice faltered with long talking Tow-a-att and Kadishan took up the story, telling what they had learned of the white man's religion; or Muir told the eager natives wonderful things about what the great one God, whose name is Love, was doing for them. The all-day meeting was only interrupted for an hour or two in the afternoon, when we walked with the chiefs across the narrow isthmus between Pyramid Harbor and the eastern arm of Lynn Canal, and I selected the harbor, farm and townsite now occupied by Haines mission and town and Fort William H. Seward. This was the beginning of the large missions of Haines and Klukwan.

THE DISCOVERY

MOONLIGHT IN GLACIER BAY

To heaven swells a mighty psalm of praise; Its music-sheets are glaciers, vast and white. Sky-piercing peaks the voiceless chorus raise, To fill with ecstasy the wond'ring night.

Complete, with every part in sweet accord, Th' adoring breezes waft it up, on wings Of beauty-incense, giving to the Lord The purest sacrifice glad Nature brings.

The list'ning stars with rapture beat and glow; The moon forgets her high, eternal calm To shout her gladness to the sea below, Whose waves are silver tongues to join the psalm.

Those everlasting snow-fields are not cold; This icy solitude no barren waste. The crystal masses burn with love untold; The glacier-table spreads a royal feast.

Fairweather! Crillon! Warders at Heaven's gate! Hoar-headed priests of Nature's inmost shrine! Strong seraph forms in robes immaculate! Draw me from earth; enlighten, change, refine;

Till I, one little note in this great song, Who seem a blot upon th'
unsullied white, No discord make--a note high, pure and strong--
Set in the silent music of the night.

IV

THE DISCOVERY

The nature-study part of the voyage was woven in with the
missionary trip as intimately as warp with woof. No island, rock,
forest, mountain or glacier which we passed, near or far, was
neglected. We went so at our own sweet will, without any set
time or schedule, that we were constantly finding objects and
points of surprise and interest. When we landed, the algæ, which
sometimes filled the little harbors, the limpets and lichens of the
rocks, the fucus pods that snapped beneath our feet, the grasses
of the beach, the moss and shrubbery among the trees, and,
more than all, the majestic forests, claimed attention and study.
Muir was one of the most expert foresters this country has ever
produced. He was never at a loss. The luxuriant vegetation of
this wet coast filled him with admiration, and he never took a
walk from camp but he had a whole volume of things to tell me,
and he was constantly bringing in trophies of which he was
prouder than any hunter of his antlers. Now it was a bunch of
ferns as high as his head; now a cluster of minute and
wonderfully beautiful moss blossoms; now a curious fungous
growth; now a spruce branch heavy with cones; and again he
would call me into the forest to see a strange and grotesque
moss formation on a dead stump, looking like a tree standing
upon its head. Thus, although his objective was the glaciers, his
thorough knowledge of botany and his interest in that study
made every camp just the place he wished to be. He always
claimed that there was more of pure ethics and even of moral
evil and good to be learned in the wilderness than from any book
or in any abode of man. He was fond of quoting Wordsworth's
stanza:

"One impulse from a vernal wood Will teach you more of man, Of moral evil and of good, Than all the sages can."

Muir was a devout theist. The Fatherhood of God and the Unity of God, the immanence of God in nature and His management of all the affairs of the universe, was his constantly reiterated belief. He saw design in many things which the ordinary naturalist overlooks, such as the symmetry of an island, the balancing branches of a tree, the harmony of colors in a group of flowers, the completion of a fully rounded landscape. In his view, the Creator of it all saw every beautiful and sublime thing from every viewpoint, and had thus formed it, not merely for His own delight, but for the delectation and instruction of His human children.

"Look at that, now," he would say, when, on turning a point, a wonderful vista of island-studded sea between mountains, with one of Alaska's matchless sunsets at the end, would wheel into sight. "Why, it looks as if these giants of God's great army had just now marched into their stations; every one placed just right, just right! What landscape gardening! What a scheme of things! And to think that He should plan to bring us feckless creatures here at the right moment, and then flash such glories at us! Man, we're not worthy of such honor!"

Thus Muir was always discovering to me things which I would never have seen myself and opening up to me new avenues of knowledge, delight and adoration. There was something so intimate in his theism that it purified, elevated and broadened mine, even when I could not agree with him. His constant exclamation when a fine landscape would burst upon our view, or a shaft of light would pierce the clouds and glorify a mountain, was, "Praise God from whom all blessings flow!"

Two or three great adventures stand out prominently in this wonderful voyage of discovery. Two weeks from home brought us to Icy Straits and the homes of the Hoonah tribe. Here the knowledge of the way on the part of our crew ended. We put into the large Hoonah village on Chichagof Island. After the usual preaching and census-taking, we took aboard a sub-chief of the Hoonahs, who was a noted seal hunter and, therefore, able to guide us among the ice-floes of the mysterious Glacier Bay of which we had heard. Vancouver's chart gave us no intimation of any inlet whatever; but the natives told of vast masses of floating ice, of a constant noise of thunder when they crashed from the glaciers into the sea; and also of fearsome bays and passages full of evil spirits which made them very perilous to navigate.

In one bay there was said to be a giant devil-fish with arms as long as a tree, lurking in malignant patience, awaiting the passage that way of an unwary canoe, when up would flash those terrible arms with their thousand suckers and, seizing their prey, would drag down the men to the bottom of the sea, there to be mangled and devoured by the horrid beak. Another deep fiord was the abode of *Koosta-kah*, the Otter-man, the mischievous Puck of Indian lore, who was waiting for voyagers to land and camp, when he would seize their sleeping forms and transport them a dozen miles in a moment, or cradle them on the tops of the highest trees. Again there was a most rapacious and ferocious killer-whale in a piece of swift water, whose delight it was to take into his great, tooth-rimmed jaws whole canoes with their crews of men, mangling them and gulping them down as a single mouthful. Many were these stories of fear told us at the Hoonah village the night before we started to explore the icy bay, and our credulous Stickeens gave us rather broad hints that it was time to turn back.

"There are no natives up in that region; there is nothing to hunt; there is no gold there; why do you persist in this *cultus coly* (aimless journey)? You are likely to meet death and nothing else if you go into that dangerous region."

All these stories made us the more eager to explore the wonders beyond, and we hastened away from Hoonah with our guide aboard. A day's sail brought us to a little, heavily wooded island near the mouth of Glacier Bay. This we named Pleasant Island.

As we broke camp in the morning our guide said: "We must take on board a supply of dry wood here, as there is none beyond."

Leaving this last green island we steered northwest into the great bay, the country of ice and bare rocks. Muir's excitement was increasing every moment, and as the majestic arena opened before us and the Muir, Geicke, Pacific and other great glaciers (all nameless as yet) began to appear, he could hardly contain himself. He was impatient of any delay, and was constantly calling to the crew to redouble their efforts and get close to these wonders. Now the marks of recent glaciation showed plainly. Here was a conical island of gray granite, whose rounded top and symmetrical shoulders were worn smooth as a Scotch monument by grinding glaciers. Here was a great mountain slashed sheer across its face, showing sharp edge and flat surface as if a slab of mountain size had been sawed from it. Yonder again loomed a granite range whose huge breasts were rounded and polished by the resistless sweep of that great ice mass which Vancouver saw filling the bay.

Soon the icebergs were charging down upon us with the receding tide and dressing up in compact phalanx when the tide arose. First would come the advance guard of smaller bergs, with here and there a house-like mass of cobalt blue with streaks of white and deeper recesses of ultra-marine; here we passed an eight-sided, solid figure of bottle-green ice; there towered an antlered formation like the horns of a stag. Now we must use all caution and give the larger icebergs a wide berth. They are treacherous creatures, these icebergs. You may be paddling along by a peaceful looking berg, sleeping on the water as mild and harmless as a lamb; when suddenly he will take a notion to turn over, and up under your canoe will come a spear of ice, impaling it and lifting it and its occupants skyward; then, turning over, down will go canoe and men to the depths.

Our progress up the sixty miles of Glacier Bay was very slow. Three nights we camped on the bare granite rock before we reached the limit of the bay. All vegetation had disappeared; hardly a bunch of grass was seen. The only signs of former life were the sodden and splintered spruce and fir stumps that projected here and there from the bases of huge gravel heaps, the moraine matter of the mighty ice mass that had engulfed them. They told the story of great forests which had once covered this whole region, until the great sea of ice of the second glacial period overwhelmed and ground them down, and buried them deep under its moraine matter. When we landed there were no level spots on which to pitch our tent and no sandy beaches or gravel beds in which to sink our tent-poles. I learned from Muir the gentle art of sleeping on a rock, curled like a squirrel around a boulder.

We passed by Muir Glacier on the other side of the bay, seeking to attain the extreme end of the great fiord. We estimated the distance by the tide and our rate of rowing, tracing the shore-line and islands as we went along and getting the points of the compass from our little pocket instrument.

Rain was falling almost constantly during the week we spent in Glacier Bay. Now and then the clouds would lift, showing the twin peaks of La Perouse and the majestic summits of Mts. Fairweather and Crillon. These mighty summits, twelve thousand, fifteen thousand and sixteen thousand feet high, respectively, pierced the sky directly above us; sometimes they seemed to be hanging over us threateningly. Only once did the sky completely clear; and then was preached to us the wonderful Sermon of Glacier Bay.

Early that morning we quitted our camp on a barren rock, steering towards Mt. Fairweather. A night of sleepless discomfort had ushered in a bleak gray morning. Our Indians were sullen and silent, their scowling looks resenting our relentless purpose to attain to the head of the bay. The air was damp and raw, chilling us to the marrow. The forbidding granite mountains, showing here and there through the fog, seemed suddenly to push out threatening fists and shoulders at us. All night long the ice-guns had bombarded us from four or five directions, when the great masses of ice from living glaciers toppled into the sea, crashing and grinding with the noise of thunder. The granite walls hurled back the sound in reiterated peals, multiplying its volume a hundredfold.

There was no Love apparent on that bleak, gray morning: Power was there in appalling force. Visions of those evergreen forests that had once clung trustingly to these mountain walls, but had been swept, one and all, by the relentless forces of the ice and buried deep under mountains of moraine matter, but added to the present desolation. We could not enjoy; we could only endure. Death from overturning icebergs, from charging tides, from mountain avalanche, threatened us.

Suddenly I heard Muir catch his breath with a fervent ejaculation. "God, Almighty!" he said. Following his gaze towards Mt. Crillon, I saw the summit highest of all crowned with glory indeed. It was not sunlight; there was no appearance of shining; it was as if the Great Artist with one sweep of His brush had laid upon the king-peak of all a crown of the most brilliant of all colors--as if a pigment, perfectly made and thickly spread, too delicate for crimson, too intense for pink, had leaped in a moment upon the mountain top; "An awful rose of dawn." The summit nearest Heaven had caught a glimpse of its glory! It was a rose blooming in ice-fields, a love-song in the midst of a stern epic, a drop from the heart of Christ upon the icy desolation and barren affections of a sin-frozen world. It warmed and thrilled us in an instant. We who had been dull and apathetic a moment before, shivering in our wet blankets, were glowing and exultant now. Even the Indians ceased their paddling, gazing with faces of awe upon the wonder. Now, as we watched that kingly peak, we saw the color leap to one and another and another of the snowy summits around it. The monarch had a whole family of royal princes about him to share his glory. Their radiant heads, ruby crowned, were above the clouds, which seemed to form their silken garments.

As we looked in ecstatic silence we saw the light creep down the mountains. It was changing now. The glowing crimson was suffused with soft, creamy light. If it was less divine, it was more warmly human. Heaven was coming down to man. The dark recesses of the mountains began to lighten. They stood forth as at the word of command from the Master of all; and as the changing mellow light moved downward that wonderful colosseum appeared clearly with its battlements and peaks and columns, until the whole majestic landscape was revealed.

Now we saw the design and purpose of it all. Now the text of this great sermon was emblazoned across the landscape--"*God is Love*"; and we understood that these relentless forces that had pushed the molten mountains heavenward, cooled them into granite peaks, covered them with snow and ice, dumped the moraine matter into the sea, filling up the sea, preparing the world for a stronger and better race of men (who knows?), were all a part of that great "All things" that "work together for good."

Our minds cleared with the landscape; our courage rose; our Indians dipped their paddles silently, steering without fear amidst the dangerous masses of ice. But there was no profanity in Muir's exclamation, "We have met with God!" A lifelong devoutness of gratitude filled us, to think that we were guided into this most wonderful room of God's great gallery, on perhaps the only day in the year when the skies were cleared and the sunrise, the atmospheric conditions and the point of view all prepared for the matchless spectacle. The discomforts of the voyage, the toil, the cold and rain of the past weeks were a small price to pay for one glimpse of its surpassing loveliness. Again and again Muir would break out, after a long silence of blissful memory, with exclamations:

"We saw it; we saw it! He sent us to His most glorious exhibition. Praise God, from whom all blessings flow!"

Two or three inspiring days followed. Muir must climb the most accessible of the mountains. My weak shoulders forbade me to ascend more than two or three thousand feet, but Muir went more than twice as high. Upon two or three of the glaciers he climbed, although the speed of these icy streams was so great and their "frozen cataracts" were so frequent, that it was difficult to ascend them.

I began to understand Muir's whole new theory, which theory made Tyndall pronounce him the greatest authority on glacial action the world had seen. He pointed out to me the mechanical laws that governed those slow-moving, resistless streams; how they carved their own valleys; how the lower valley and glacier were often the resultant in size and velocity of the two or three glaciers that now formed the branches of the main glaciers; how the harder strata of rock resisted and turned the masses of ice; how the steely ploughshares were often inserted into softer leads and a whole mountain split apart as by a wedge.

Muir would explore all day long, often rising hours before daylight and disappearing among the mountains, not coming to camp until after night had fallen. Again and again the Indians said that he was lost; but I had no fears for him. When he would return to camp he was so full of his discoveries and of the new facts garnered that he would talk until long into the night, almost forgetting to eat.

Returning down the bay, we passed the largest glacier of all, which was to bear Muir's name. It was then fully a mile and a half in width, and the perpendicular face of it towered from four to seven hundred feet above the surface of the water. The ice masses were breaking off so fast that we were forced to put off far from the face of the glacier. The great waves threatened constantly to dash us against the sharp points of the icebergs. We wished to land and scale the glacier from the eastern side. We rowed our canoe about half a mile from the edge of the glacier, but, attempting to land, were forced hastily to put off again. A great wave, formed by the masses of ice breaking off into the water, threatened to dash our loaded canoe against the boulders on the beach. Rowing further away, we tried it again and again, with the same result. As soon as we neared the shore another huge wave would threaten destruction. We were fully a mile and a half from the edge of the glacier before we found it safe to land.

[Illustration: MUIR GLACIER

Returning down Glacier Bay, we visited the largest glacier of all, which was to bear Muir's name]

Muir spent a whole day alone on the glacier, walking over twenty miles across what he called the glacial lake between two mountains. A cold, penetrating, mist-like rain was falling, and dark clouds swept up the bay and clung about the shoulders of the mountains. When night approached and Muir had not returned, I set the Indians to digging out from the bases of the gravel hills the frazzled stumps and logs that remained of the buried forests. These were full of resin and burned brightly. I made a great fire and cooked a good supper of venison, beans, biscuit and coffee. When pitchy darkness gathered, and still Muir did not come, Tow-a-att made some torches of fat spruce, and taking with him Charley, laden with more wood, he went up the beach a mile and a half, climbed the base of the mountain and kindled a beacon which flashed its cheering rays far over the glacier.

Muir came stumbling into camp with these two Indians a little before midnight, very tired but very happy. "Ah!" he sighed, "I'm glad to be in camp. The glacier almost got me this time. If it had not been for the beacon and old Tow-a-att, I might have had to spend the night on the ice. The crevasses were so many and so bewildering in their mazy, crisscross windings that I was actually going farther into the glacier when I caught the flash of light."

I brought him to the tent and placed the hot viands before him. He attacked them ravenously, but presently was talking again:

"Man, man; you ought to have been with me. You'll never make up what you have lost to-day. I've been wandering through a thousand rooms of God's crystal temple. I've been a thousand feet down in the crevasses, with matchless domes and sculptured figures and carved ice-work all about me. Solomon's marble and ivory palaces were nothing to it. Such purity, such color, such delicate beauty! I was tempted to stay there and feast my soul, and softly freeze, until I would become part of the glacier. What a great death that would be!"

Again and again I would have to remind Muir that he was eating his supper, but it was more than an hour before I could get him to finish the meal, and two or three hours longer before he stopped talking and went to sleep. I wish I had taken down his descriptions. What splendid reading they would make!

But scurries of snow warned us that winter was coming, and, much to the relief of our natives, we turned the prow of our canoe towards Chatham Strait again. Landing our Hoonah guide at his village, we took our route northward again up Lynn Canal. The beautiful Davison Glacier with its great snowy fan drew our gaze and excited our admiration for two days; then the visit to the Chilcats and the return trip commenced. Bowling down the canal before a strong north wind, we entered Stevens Passage, and visited the two villages of the Auk Indians, a squalid, miserable tribe. We camped at the site of what is now Juneau, the capital of Alaska, and no dream of the millions of gold that were to be taken from those mountains disturbed us. If we had known, I do not think that we would have halted a day or staked a claim. Our treasures were richer than gold and securely laid up in the vaults of our memories.

An excursion into Taku Bay, that miniature of Glacier Bay, with its then three living glaciers; a visit to two villages of the Taku Indians; past Ft. Snettisham, up whose arms we pushed, mapping them; then to Sumdum. Here the two arms of Holkham Bay, filled with ice, enticed us to exploration, but the constant rains of the fall had made the ice of the glaciers more viscid and the glacier streams more rapid; hence the vast array of icebergs charging down upon us like an army, spreading out in loose formation and then gathering into a barrier when the tide turned, made exploration to the end of the bay impossible. Muir would not give up his quest of the mother glacier until the Indians frankly refused to go any further; and old Tow-a-att called our interpreter, Johnny, as for a counsel of state, and carefully set forth to Muir that if he persisted in his purpose of pushing forward up the bay he would have the blood of the whole party on his hands.

Said the old chief: "My life is of no account, and it does not matter whether I live or die; but you shall not sacrifice the life of my minister."

I laughed at Muir's discomfiture and gave the word to retreat. This one defeat of a victorious expedition so weighed upon Muir's mind that it brought him back from the California coast next year and from the arms of his bride to discover and climb upon that glacier.

On down now through Prince Frederick Sound, past the beautiful Norris Glacier, then into Le Conte Bay with its living glacier and icebergs, across the Stickeen flats, and so joyfully home again, Muir to take the November steamboat back to his sunland.

I have made many voyages in that great Alexandrian Archipelago since, traveling by canoe over fifteen thousand miles--not one of them a dull one--through its intricate passages; but none compared, in the number and intensity of its thrills, in the variety and excitement of its incidents and in its lasting impressions of beauty and grandeur, with this first voyage when we groped our way northward with only Vancouver's old chart as our guide.

THE LOST GLACIER

NIGHT IN A CANOE

A dreary world! The constant rain Beats back to earth blithe fancy's wings; And life--a sodden garment--clings About a body numb with pain.

Imagination ceased with light; Of Nature's psalm no echo lingers. The death-cold mist, with ghostly fingers, Shrouds world and soul in rayless night.

An inky sea, a sullen crew, A frail canoe's uncertain motion; A whispered talk of wind and ocean, As plotting secret crimes to do!

The vampire-night sucks all my blood; Warm home and love seem lost for aye; From cloud to cloud I steal away, Like guilty soul o'er Stygian flood.

Peace, morbid heart! From paddle blade See the black water flash in light; And bars of moonbeams streaming white, Have pearls of ebon raindrops made.

From darkest sea of deep despair Gleams Hope, awaked by
Action's blow; And Faith's clear ray, though clouds hang low,
Slants up to heights serene and fair.

V

THE LOST GLACIER

John Muir was married in the spring of 1880 to Miss Strentzel,
the daughter of a Polish physician who had come out in the great
stampede of 1849 to California, but had found his gold in
oranges, lemons and apricots on a great fruit ranch at Martinez,
California. A brief letter from Muir told of his marriage, with just
one note in it, the depth of joy and peace of which I could
fathom, knowing him so well. Then no word of him until the
monthly mailboat came in September. As I stood on the wharf
with the rest of the Wrangell population, as was the custom of
our isolation, watching the boat come in, I was overjoyed to see
John Muir on deck, in that same old, long, gray ulster and Scotch
cap. He waved and shouted at me before the boat touched the
wharf.

Springing ashore he said, "When can you be ready?"

"Aren't you a little fast?" I replied. "What does this mean?
Where's your wife?"

"Man," he exclaimed, "have you forgotten? Don't you know we
lost a glacier last fall? Do you think I could sleep soundly in my
bed this winter with that hanging on my conscience? My wife
could not come, so I have come alone and you've got to go with
me to find the lost. Get your canoe and crew and let us be off."

The ten months since Muir had left me had not been spent in idleness at Wrangell. I had made two long voyages of discovery and missionary work on my own account,--one in the spring, of four hundred fifty miles around Prince of Wales Island, visiting the five towns of Hydah Indians and the three villages of the Hanega tribe of Thlingets. Another in the summer down the coast to the Cape Fox and Tongass tribes of Thlingets, and across Dixon entrance to Ft. Simpson, where there was a mission among the Tsimpheans, and on fifteen miles further to the famous mission of Father Duncan at Metlakahtla. I had written accounts of these trips to Muir; but for him the greatest interest was in the glaciers and mountains of the mainland.

Our preparations were soon made. Alas! we could not have our noble old captain, Tow-a-att, this time. On the tenth of January, 1880,--the darkest day of my life,--this "noblest Roman of them all" fell dead at my feet with a bullet through his forehead, shot by a member of that same Hootz-noo tribe where he had preached the gospel of peace so simply and eloquently a few months before. The Hootz-noos, maddened by the fiery liquor that bore their name, came to Wrangell, and a preliminary skirmish led to an attack at daylight of that winter day upon the Stickeen village. Old Tow-a-att had stood for peace, and rather than have any bloodshed had offered all his blankets as a peace offering, although in no physical fear himself; but when the Hootz-noos, encouraged by the seeming cowardice of the Stickeens, broke into their houses, and the Christianized tribe, provoked beyond endurance, came out with their guns, Tow-a-att came forth armed only with his old carved spear, the emblem of his position as chief, to see if he could not call his tribe back again. At my instance, as I stood with my hand on his shoulder, he lifted up his voice to recall his people to their houses, when, in an instant, the volley commenced on both sides, and this Christian man, one of the simplest and grandest souls I ever knew, fell dead at my feet, and the tribe was tumbled back into barbarism; and the white man, who had taught the

Indians the art of making rum, and the white man's government, which had afforded no safeguard against such scenes, were responsible.

[Illustration: DAVIDSON GLACIER

The beautiful Davidson Glacier, with its great snow-white fan, drew our gaze and excited our admiration for two days]

Muir mourned with me the fate of this old chief; but another of my men, Lot Tyeen, was ready with a swift canoe. Joe, his son-in-law, and Billy Dickinson, a half-breed boy of seventeen who acted as interpreter, formed the crew. When we were about to embark I suddenly thought of my little dog Stickeen and made the resolve to take him along. My wife and Muir both protested and I almost yielded to their persuasion. I shudder now to think what the world would have lost had their arguments prevailed! That little, long-haired, brisk, beautiful, but very independent dog, in co-ordination with Muir's genius, was to give to the world one of its greatest dog-classics. Muir's story of "Stickeen" ranks with "Rab and His Friends," "Bob, Son of Battle," and far above "The Call of the Wild." Indeed, in subtle analysis of dog character, as well as beauty of description, I think it outranks all of them. All over the world men, women and children are reading with laughter, thrills and tears this exquisite little story.

I have told Muir that in his book he did not do justice to my puppy's beauty. I think that he was the handsomest dog I have ever known. His markings were very much like those of an American Shepherd dog--black, white and tan; although he was not half the size of one; but his hair was so silky and so long, his tail so heavily fringed and beautifully curved, his eyes so deep and expressive and his shape so perfect in its graceful contours, that I have never seen another dog quite like him; otherwise Muir's description of him is perfect.

When Stickeen was only a round ball of silky fur as big as one's fist, he was given as a wedding present to my bride, two years before this voyage. I carried him in my overcoat pocket to and from the steamer as we sailed from Sitka to Wrangell. Soon after we arrived a solemn delegation of Stickeen Indians came to call on the bride; but as soon as they saw the puppy they were solemn no longer. His gravely humorous antics were irresistible. It was Moses who named him Stickeen after their tribe--an exceptional honor. Thereafter the whole tribe adopted and protected him, and woe to the Indian dog which molested him. Once when I was passing the house of this same Lot Tyeen, one of his large hunting dogs dashed out at Stickeen and began to worry him. Lot rescued the little fellow, delivered him to me and walked into his house. Soon he came out with his gun, and before I knew what he was about he had shot the offending Indian dog--a valuable hunting animal.

Stickeen lacked the obtrusively affectionate manner of many of his species, did not like to be fussed over, would even growl when our babies enmeshed their hands in his long hair; and yet, to a degree I have never known in another dog, he attracted the attention of everybody and won all hearts.

As instances: Dr. Kendall, "The Grand Old Man" of our Church, during his visit of 1879 used to break away from solemn counsels with the other D.D.s and the carpenters to run after and shout at Stickeen. And Mrs. McFarland, the Mother of Protestant missions in Alaska, often begged us to give her the dog; and, when later he was stolen from her care by an unscrupulous tourist and so forever lost to us, she could hardly afterwards speak of him without tears.

Stickeen was a born aristocrat, dainty and scrupulously clean. From puppyhood he never cared to play with the Indian dogs, and I was often amused to see the dignified but decided way in which he repulsed all attempts at familiarity on the part of the

Indian children. He admitted to his friendship only a few of the natives, choosing those who had adopted the white man's dress and mode of living, and were devoid of the rank native odors. His likes and dislikes were very strong and always evident from the moment of his meeting with a stranger. There was something almost uncanny about the accuracy of his judgment when "sizing up" a man.

It was Stickeen himself who really decided the question whether we should take him with us on this trip. He listened to the discussion, pro and con, as he stood with me on the wharf, turning his sharp, expressive eyes and sensitive ears up to me or down to Muir in the canoe. When the argument seemed to be going against the dog he suddenly turned, deliberately walked down the gang-plank to the canoe, picked his steps carefully to the bow, where my seat with Muir was arranged, and curled himself down on my coat. The discussion ended abruptly in a general laugh, and Stickeen went along.

Then the acute little fellow set about, in the wisest possible way, to conquer Muir. He was not obtrusive, never "butted in"; never offended by a too affectionate tongue. He listened silently to discussions on his merits, those first days; but when Muir's comparisons of the brilliant dogs of his acquaintance with Stickeen grew too "odious" Stickeen would rise, yawn openly and retire to a distance, not slinkingly, but with tail up, and lie down again out of earshot of such calumnies. When we landed after a day's journey Stickeen was always the first ashore, exploring for field mice and squirrels; but when we would start to the woods, the mountains or the glaciers the dog would join us, coming mysteriously from the forest. When our paths separated, Stickeen, looking to me for permission, would follow Muir, trotting at first behind him, but gradually ranging alongside.

After a few days Muir changed his tone, saying, "There's more in that wee beastie than I thought"; and before a week passed

Stickeen's victory was complete; he slept at Muir's feet, went with him on all his rambles; and even among dangerous crevasses or far up the steep slopes of granite mountains the little dog's splendid tail would be seen ahead of Muir, waving cheery signals to his new-found human companion.

Our canoe was light and easily propelled. Our outfit was very simple, for this was to be a quick voyage and there were not to be so many missionary visits this time. It was principally a voyage of discovery; we were in search of the glacier that we had lost. Perched in the high stern sat our captain, Lot Tyeen, massive and capable, handling his broad steering paddle with power and skill. In front of him Joe and Billy pulled oars, Joe, a strong young man, our cook, hunter and best oarsman; Billy, a lad of seventeen, our interpreter and Joe's assistant. Towards the bow, just behind the mast, sat Muir and I, each with a paddle in his hands. Stickeen slumbered at our feet or gazed into our faces when our conversation interested him. When we began to discuss a landing place he would climb the high bow and brace himself on the top of the beak, an animated figure-head, ready to jump into the water when we were about to camp.

Our route was different from that of '79. Now we struck through Wrangell Narrows, that tortuous and narrow passage between Mitkof and Kupreanof Islands, past Norris Glacier with its far-flung shaft of ice appearing above the forests as if suspended in air; past the bold Pt. Windham with its bluff of three thousand feet frowning upon the waters of Prince Frederick Sound; across Port Houghton, whose deep fiord had no ice in it and, therefore, was not worthy of an extended visit. We made all haste, for Muir was, as the Indians said, "always hungry for ice," and this was more especially his expedition. He was the commander now, as I had been the year before. He had set for himself the limit of a month and must return by the October boat. Often we ran until late at night against the protests of our Indians, whose life of infinite leisure was not accustomed to such rude interruption.

They could not understand Muir at all, nor in the least comprehend his object in visiting icy bays where there was no chance of finding gold and nothing to hunt.

The vision rises before me, as my mind harks back to this second trip of seven hundred miles, of cold, rainy nights, when, urged by Muir to make one more point, the natives passed the last favorable camping place and we blindly groped for hours in pitchy darkness, trying to find a friendly beach. The intensely phosphorescent water flashed about us, the only relief to the inky blackness of the night. Occasionally a salmon or a big halibut, disturbed by our canoe, went streaming like a meteor through the water, throwing off coruscations of light. As we neared the shore, the waves breaking upon the rocks furnished us the only illumination. Sometimes their black tops with waving seaweed, surrounded by phosphorescent breakers, would have the appearance of mouths set with gleaming teeth rushing at us out of the dark as if to devour us. Then would come the landing on a sandy beach, the march through the seaweed up to the wet woods, a fusillade of exploding fucus pods accompanying us as if the outraged fairies were bombarding us with tiny guns. Then would ensue a tedious groping with the lantern for a camping place and for some dry, fat spruce wood from which to coax a fire; then the big camp-fire, the bean-pot and coffee-pot, the cheerful song and story, and the deep, dreamless sleep that only the weary voyageur or hunter can know.

Four or five days sufficed to bring us to our first objective--Sumdum or Holkham Bay, with its three wonderful arms. Here we were to find the lost glacier. This deep fiord has two great prongs. Neither of them figured in Vancouver's chart, and so far as records go we were the first to enter and follow to its end the longest of these, Endicott Arm. We entered the bay at night, caught again by the darkness, and groped our way uncertainly. We probably would have spent most of the night trying to find a landing place had not the gleam of a fire greeted us, flashing through the trees, disappearing as an island intervened, and again opening up with its fair ray as we pushed on. An hour's steady paddling brought us to the camp of some Cassiar miners--my friends. They were here at the foot of a glacier stream, from the bed of which they had been sluicing gold. Just now they were in hard luck, as the constant rains had swelled the glacial stream, burst through their wing-dams, swept away their sluice-boxes and destroyed the work of the summer. Strong men of the wilderness as they were, they were not discouraged, but were discussing plans for prospecting new places and trying it again here next summer. Hot coffee and fried venison emphasized their welcome, and we in return could give them a little news from the outside world, from which they had been shut off completely for months.

Muir called us before daylight the next morning. He had been up since two or three o'clock, "studying the night effects," he said, listening to the roaring and crunching of the charging ice as it came out of Endicott Arm, spreading out like the skirmish line of an army and grinding against the rocky point just below us. He had even attempted a moonlight climb up the sloping face of a high promontory with Stickeen as his companion, but was unable to get to the top, owing to the smoothness of the granite rock. It was newly glaciated--this whole region--and the hard rubbing ice-tools had polished the granite like a monument. A hasty meal and we were off.

"We'll find it this time," said Muir.

A miner crawled out of his blankets and came to see us start. "If it's scenery you're after," he said, "ten miles up the bay there's the nicest canyon you ever saw. It has no name that I know of, but it is sure some scenery."

The long, straight fiord stretched southeast into the heart of the granite range, its funnel shape producing tremendous tides.

When the tide was ebbing that charging phalanx of ice was irresistible, storming down the canyon with race-horse speed; no canoe could stem that current. We waited until the turn, then getting inside the outer fleet of icebergs we paddled up with the flood tide. Mile after mile we raced past those smooth mountain shoulders; higher and higher they towered, and the ice, closing in upon us, threatened a trap. The only way to navigate safely that dangerous fiord was to keep ahead of the charging ice. As we came up towards the end of the bay the narrowing walls of the fiord compressed the ice until it crowded dangerously around us. Our captain, Lot, had taken the precaution to put a false bow and stern on his canoe, cunningly fashioned out of curved branches of trees and hollowed with his hand-adz to fit the ends of the canoe. These were lashed to the bow and stern by thongs of deer sinew. They were needed. It was like penetrating an arctic ice-floe. Sometimes we would have to skirt the granite rock and with our poles shove out the ice-cakes to secure a passage. It was fully thirty miles to the head of the bay, but we made it in half a day, so strong was the current of the rising tide.

I shall never forget the view that burst upon us as we rounded the last point. The face of the glacier where it discharged its icebergs was very narrow in comparison with the giants of Glacier Bay, but the ice cliff was higher than even the face of Muir Glacier. The narrow canyon of hard granite had compressed the ice of the great glacier until it had the appearance of a frozen torrent broken into innumerable crevasses, the great masses of ice tumbling over one another and bulging out for a few moments before they came crashing and splashing down into the deep water of the bay. The fiord was simply a cleft in high mountains, and the depth of the water could only be conjectured. It must have been hundreds of feet, perhaps thousands, from the surface of the water to the bottom of that fissure. Smooth, polished, shining breasts of bright gray granite crowded above the glacier on every side, seeming to overhang the ice and the bay. Struggling clumps of evergreens clung to the mountain sides below the glacier, and up, away up, dizzily to the sky towered the walls of the canyon. Hundreds of other Alaskan glaciers excel this in masses of ice and in grandeur of front, but none that I have seen condense beauty and grandeur to finer results.

"What a plucky little giant!" was Muir's exclamation as we stood on a rock-mound in front of this glacier. "To think of his shouldering his way through the mountain range like this! Samson, pushing down the pillars of the temple at Gaza, was nothing to this fellow. Hear him roar and laugh!"

Without consulting me Muir named this "Young Glacier," and right proud was I to see that name on the charts for the next ten years or more, for we mapped Endicott Arm and the other arm of Sumdum Bay as we had Glacier Bay; but later maps have a different name. Some ambitious young ensign on a surveying vessel, perhaps, stole my glacier, and later charts give it the name of Dawes. I have not found in the Alaskan statute books any penalty attached to the crime of stealing a glacier, but certainly it ought to be ranked as a felony of the first magnitude, the grandest of grand larcenies.

A couple of days and nights spent in the vicinity of Young Glacier were a period of unmixed pleasure. Muir spent all of these days and part of the nights climbing the pinnacled mountains to this and that viewpoint, crossing the deep, narrow and dangerous glacier five thousand feet above the level of the sea, exploring its tributaries and their side canyons, making sketches in his note-book for future elaboration. Stickeen by this time constantly followed Muir, exciting my jealousy by his plainly expressed preference. Because of my bad shoulder the higher and steeper ascents of this very rugged region were impossible to me, and I must content myself with two thousand feet and even lesser climbs. My favorite perch was on the summit of a sugar-loaf rock which formed the point of a promontory jutting into the bay directly in front of my glacier, and distant from its face less than a quarter of a mile. It was a granite fragment which had evidently been broken off from the mountain; indeed, there was a niche five thousand feet above into which it would exactly fit. The sturdy evergreens struggled half-way up its sides, but the top was bare.

On this splendid pillar I spent many hours. Generally I could see Muir, fortunate in having sound arms and legs, scaling the high rock-faces, now coming out on a jutting spur, now spread like a spider against the mountain wall. Here he would be botanizing in a patch of green that relieved the gray of the granite, there he was dodging in and out of the blue crevasses of the upper glacial falls. Darting before him or creeping behind was a little black speck which I made out to be Stickeen, climbing steeps up which a fox would hardly venture. Occasionally I would see him dancing about at the base of a cliff too steep for him, up which Muir was climbing, and his piercing howls of protest at being left behind would come echoing down to me.

But chiefly I was engrossed in the great drama which was being acted before me by the glacier itself. It was the battle of gravity with flinty hardness and strong cohesion. The stage setting was perfect; the great hall formed by encircling mountains; the side curtains of dark-green forest, fold on fold; the gray and brown top-curtains of the mountain heights stretching clear across the glacier, relieved by vivid moss and flower patches of yellow, magenta, violet and crimson. But the face of the glacier was so high and rugged and the ice so pure that it showed a variety of blue and purple tints I have never seen surpassed--baby-blue, sky-blue, sapphire, turquoise, cobalt, indigo, peacock, ultra-marine, shading at the top into lilac and amethyst. The base of the glacier-face, next to the dark-green water of the bay, resembled a great mass of vitriol, while the top, where it swept out of the canyon, had the curves and tints and delicate lines of the iris.

[Illustration: TAKU GLACIER

There followed an excursion into Taku Bay, that miniature of Glacier Bay, with its three living glaciers]

But the glacier front was not still; in form and color it was changing every minute. The descent was so steep that the glacial rapids above the bay must have flowed forward eighty or a hundred feet a day. The ice cliff, towering a thousand feet over the water, would present a slight incline from the perpendicular inwards toward the canyon, the face being white from powdered ice, the result of the grinding descent of the ice masses. Here and there would be little cascades of this fine ice spraying out as they fell, with glints of prismatic colors when the sunlight struck them. As I gazed I could see the whole upper part of the cliff slowly moving forward until the ice-face was vertical. Then, foot by foot it would be pushed out until the upper edge overhung the water. Now the outer part, denuded of the ice powder, would present a face of delicate blue with darker shades where the mountain peaks cast their shadows. Suddenly from top to bottom of the ice cliff two deep lines of prussian blue appeared. They were crevasses made by the ice current flowing more rapidly in the center of the stream. Fascinated, I watched this great pyramid of blue-veined onyx lean forward until it became a tower of Pisa, with fragments falling thick and fast from its upper apex and from the cliffs out of which it had been split. Breathless and anxious, I awaited the final catastrophe, and its long delay became almost a greater strain than I could bear. I jumped up and down and waved my arms and shouted at the glacier to "hurry up."

Suddenly the climax came in a surprising way. The great tower of crystal shot up into the air two hundred feet or more, impelled by the pressure of a hundred fathoms of water, and then, toppling over, came crashing into the water with a roar as of rending mountains. Its weight of thousands of tons, falling from such a height, splashed great sheets of water high into the air, and a rainbow of wondrous brilliance flashed and vanished. A mighty wave swept majestically down the bay, rocking the massive bergs like corks, and, breaking against my granite pillar, tossed its spray half-way up to my lofty perch. Muir's shout of applause and Stickeen's sharp bark came faintly to my ears when the deep rumbling of the newly formed icebergs had subsided.

That night I waited supper long for Muir. It was a good supper--a mulligan stew of mallard duck, with biscuits and coffee. Stickeen romped into camp about ten o'clock and his new master soon followed.

"Ah!" sighed Muir between sips of coffee, "what a Lord's mercy it is that we lost this glacier last fall, when we were pressed for time, to find it again in these glorious days that have flashed out of the mists for our special delectation. This has been a day of days. I have found four new varieties of moss, and have learned many new and wonderful facts about world-shaping. And then, the wonder and glory! Why, all the values of beauty and sublimity--form, color, motion and sound--have been present to-day at their very best. My friend, we are the richest men in all the world to-night."

Charging down the canyon with the charging ice on our return, we kept to the right-hand shore, on the watch for the mouth of the canyon of "some scenery." We had not been able to discover it from the other side as we ascended the fiord. We were almost swept past the mouth of it by the force of the current. Paddling into an eddy, we were suddenly halted as if by a strong hand pushed against the bow, for the current was flowing like a cataract out of the narrow mouth of this side canyon. A rocky shelf afforded us a landing place. We hastily unloaded the canoe and pulled it up upon the beach out of reach of the floating ice, and there we had to wait until the next morning before we could penetrate the depths of this great canyon.

We shot through the mouth of the canyon at dangerous speed. Indeed, we could not do otherwise; we were helpless in the grasp of the torrent. At certain stages the surging tide forms an actual fall, for the entrance is so narrow that the water heaps up and pours over. We took the beginning of the flood tide, and so escaped that danger; but our speed must have been, at the narrows, twenty miles an hour. Then, suddenly, the bay widened out, the water ceased to swirl and boil and the current became gentle.

When we could lay aside our paddles and look up, one of the most glorious views of the whole world "smote us in the face," and Muir's chant arose, "Praise God from whom all blessings flow."

Before entering this bay I had expressed a wish to see Yosemite Valley. Now Muir said: "There is your Yosemite; only this one is on much the grander scale. Yonder towers El Capitan, grown to twice his natural size; there are the Sentinel, and the majestic Dome; and see all the falls. Those three have some resemblance to Yosemite Falls, Nevada and Bridal Veil; but the mountain breasts from which they leap are much higher than in Yosemite, and the sheer drop much greater. And there are so many more of these and they fall into the sea. We'll call this Yosemite Bay--a bigger Yosemite, as Alaska is bigger than California."

Two very beautiful glaciers lay at the head of this canyon. They did not descend to the water, but the narrow strip of moraine matter without vegetation upon it between the glaciers and the bay showed that it had not been long since they were glaciers of the first class, sending out a stream of icebergs to join those from the Young Glacier. These glaciers stretched away miles and miles, like two great antennæ, from the head of the bay to the top of the mountain range. But the most striking features of this scene were the wonderfully rounded and polished granite breasts of these great heights. In one stretch of about a mile on either side of the narrow bay parallel mouldings, like massive cornices of gray granite, five or six thousand feet high, overhung the water. These had been fluted and rounded and polished by the glacier stream, until they seemed like the upper walls and Corinthian capitals of a great temple. The power of the ice stream could be seen in the striated shoulders of these cliffs. What awful force that tool of steel-like ice must have possessed, driven by millions of tons of weight, to mould and shape and scoop out these flinty rock faces, as the carpenter's forming plane flutes a board!

When we were half-way up this wonderful bay the sun burst through a rift of cloud. "Look, look!" exclaimed Muir. "Nature is turning on the colored lights in her great show house."

Instantly this severe, bare hall of polished rock was transformed into a fairy palace. A score of cascades, the most of them invisible before, leapt into view, falling from the dizzy mountain heights and spraying into misty veils as they descended; and from all of them flashed rainbows of marvelous distinctness and brilliance, waving and dancing--a very riot of color. The tinkling water falling into the bay waked a thousand echoes, weird, musical and sweet, a riot of sound. It was an enchanted palace, and we left it with reluctance, remaining only six hours and going out at the turn of the flood tide to escape the dangerous rapids. Had there not been any so many things to see beyond, and so little time in which to see them, I doubt if Muir would have quit Yosemite Bay for days.

THE DOG AND THE MAN

MY FRIENDS

Two friends I have, and close akin are they. For both are free
And wild and proud, full of the ecstasy Of life untrammeled;
living, day by day, A law unto themselves; yet breaking none Of
Nature's perfect code. And far afield, remote from man's abode,
They roam the wilds together, two as one.

Yet, one's a dog--a wisp of silky hair, Two sharp black eyes, A
face alert, mysterious and wise, A shadowy tail, a body lithe and
fair. And one's a man--of Nature's work the best, A heart of gold,
A mind stored full of treasures new and old, Of men the greatest,
strongest, tenderest.

They love each other--these two friends of mine-- Yet both agree
In this--with that pure love that's half divine They both love me.

VI

THE DOG AND THE MAN

There is no time to tell of all the bays we explored; of Holkham
Bay, Port Snettisham, Tahkou Harbor; all of which we rudely put
on the map, or at least extended the arms beyond what was
previously known. Through Gastineau Channel, now famous for
some of the greatest quartz mines and mills in the world, we
pushed, camping on the site of what is now Juneau, the capital
city of Alaska.

An interesting bit of history is to be recorded here. Pushing
across the flats at the head of the bay at high tide the next
morning (for the narrow, grass-covered flat between Gastineau
Channel and Stevens Passage can only be crossed with canoes
at flood tide), we met two old gold prospectors whom I had
frequently seen at Wrangell--Joe Harris and Joe Juneau.
Exchanging greetings and news, they told us they were out from
Sitka on a leisurely hunting and prospecting trip. Asking us about
our last camping place, Harris said to Juneau, "Suppose we

camp there and try the gravel of that creek."

These men found placer gold and rock "float" at our camp and made quite a clean-up that fall, returning to Sitka with a "gold-poke" sufficiently plethoric to start a stampede to the new diggings. Both placer and quartz locations were made and a brisk "camp" was built the next summer. This town was first called Harrisburg for one of the prospectors, and afterwards Juneau for the other. The great Treadwell gold quartz mine was located three miles from Juneau in 1881, and others subsequently. The territorial capital was later removed from Sitka to Juneau, and the city has grown in size and importance, until it is one of the great mining and commercial centers of the Northwest.

Through Stevens Passage we paddled, stopping to preach to the Auk Indians; then down Chatham Strait and into Icy Strait, where the crystal masses of Muir and Pacific glaciers flashed a greeting from afar. We needed no Hoonah guide this time, and it was well we did not, for both Hoonah villages were deserted. The inhabitants had gone to their hunting, fishing or berry-picking grounds.

At Pleasant Island we loaded, as on the previous trip, with dry wood for our voyage into Glacier Bay. We were not to attempt the head of the bay this time, but to confine our exploration to Muir Glacier, which we had only touched upon the previous fall. Pleasant Island was the scene of one of Stickeen's many escapades. The little island fairly teemed with big field mice and pine squirrels, and Stickeen went wild. We could hear his shrill bark, now here, now there, from all parts of the island. When we were ready to leave the next morning he was not to be seen. We got aboard as usual, thinking that he would follow. A quarter of a mile's paddling and still no little black head could be discovered in our wake. Muir, who was becoming very much attached to the little dog, was plainly worried.

"Row back," he said.

So we rowed back and called, but no Stickeen. Around the next point we rowed and whistled; still no Stickeen. At last, discouraged, I gave the signal to move off. So we rounded the curving shore and pushed towards Glacier Bay. At the far point of the island, a mile from our camping place, we suddenly discovered Stickeen away out in the water, paddling calmly and confidently towards our canoe. How he had ever got there I cannot imagine. I think he must have been taking a long swim out on the bay for the mere pleasure of it. Muir always insisted that he had listened to our discussion of the route to be taken, and, with an uncanny intuition that approached clairvoyance, knew just where to head us off.

When we took him aboard he went through his usual performance, making his way, the whole length of the canoe, until he got under Muir's legs, before shaking himself. No protests or discipline availed, for Muir's kicks always failed of their pretended mark. To the end of his acquaintance with Muir, he always chose the vicinity of Muir's legs as the place to shake himself after a swim.

At Muir Glacier we spent a week this time, making long trips up the mountains that overlooked the glacier and across its surface. On one occasion Muir, with the little dog at his heels, crossed entirely in a diagonal direction the great glacial lake, a trip of some thirty miles, starting before daylight in the morning and not appearing at camp until long after dark. Muir always carried several handkerchiefs in his pockets, but this time he returned without any, having used them all up making moccasins for Stickeen, whose feet were cut and bleeding from the sharp honeycomb ice of the glacial surface. This mass of ice is so vast and so comparatively still that it has but few crevasses, and Muir's day for traversing it was a perfect one--warm and sunny.

[Illustration: THE FRONT OF MUIR GLACIER

We could understand the constant breaking off and leaping up and smashing down of the ice, and the formation of the great mass of bergs]

Another day he and I climbed the mountain that overlooked it and skirted the mighty ice-field for some distance, then walked across the face of the glacier just back of the rapids, keeping away from the deep crevasses. We drove a straight line of stakes across the glacial stream and visited them each day to watch the deflection and curves of the stakes, and thus arrive at some conception of the rate at which the ice mass was moving. In some parts of the glacial stream this ice current flowed as fast as fifty or sixty feet a day, and we could understand the constant breaking off and leaping up and smashing down of the ice and the formation of that great mass of bergs.

Shortly before we left Muir Glacier, I saw Muir furiously angry for the first and last time in my acquaintance with him. We had noticed day after day, whenever the mists admitted a view of the mountain slopes, bands of mountain goats looking like little white mice against the green of the high pastures. I said to Joe, the hunter, one morning: "Go up and get us a kid. It will be a great addition to our larder."

He took my breech-loading rifle and went. In the afternoon he returned with a fine young buck on his shoulders. While we were examining it he said:

"I picked the fattest and most tender of those that I killed."

"What!" I exclaimed, "did you kill more than this one?"

He put up both hands with fingers extended and then one finger:

"*Tatlum-pe-ict* (eleven)," he replied.

Muir's face flushed red, and with an exclamation that was as near to an oath as he ever came, he started for Joe. Luckily for that Indian he saw Muir and fled like a deer up the rocks, and would not come down until he was assured that he would not be hurt. I shared Muir's indignation and would have enjoyed seeing him administer the richly deserved thrashing.

Muir had a strong aversion to taking the life of any animal; although he would eat meat when prepared, he never killed a wild animal; even the rattlesnakes he did not molest during his rambles in California. Often his softness of heart was a source of some annoyance and a great deal of astonishment to our natives; for he would take pleasure in rocking the canoe when they were trying to get a bead on a flock of ducks or a deer standing on the shore.

On leaving the mouth of Glacier Bay we spent a week or more exploring the inlets and glaciers to the west. These days were rainy and cold. We groped blindly into unknown, unmapped, fog-hidden fiords and bayous, exploring them to their ends and often making excursions to the glaciers above them.

The climax of the trip, however, was the last glacier we visited, Taylor Glacier, the scene of Muir's great adventure with Stickeen. We reached this fine glacier in the afternoon of a very stormy day. We were approaching the open Pacific, and the *saanah*, the southeast rain-wind, was howling through the narrow entrance into Cross Sound. For twenty miles we had been facing strong head winds and tidal waves as we crept around rocky points and along the bases of dizzy cliffs and glacier-scored rock-shoulders. We were drenched to the skin; indeed, our clothing and blankets had been soaking wet for days. For two hours before we turned the point into the cozy harbor in front of the glacier we had been exerting every ounce of our strength; Lot in the stern wielding his big steering paddle, now on this side, now on that, grunting with each mighty stroke, calling encouragement to his crew, "*Ut-ha, ut-ha! hlitsin! hlitsin-tin!* (pull, pull, strong, with strength!)"; Joe and Billy rising from their seats with every stroke and throwing their whole weight and force savagely into their oars; Muir and I in the bow bent forward with heads down, butting into the slashing rain, paddling for dear life; Stickeen, the only idle one, looking over the side of the boat as though searching the channel and then around at us as if he would like to help. All except the dog were exhausted when we turned into the sheltered cove.

While the men pitched the tents and made camp Muir and I walked through the thick grass to the front of the large glacier, which front stretched from a high, perpendicular rock wall about three miles to a narrow promontory of moraine boulders next to the ocean.

"Now, here is something new," exclaimed Muir, as we stood close to the edge of the ice. "This glacier is the great exception. All the others of this region are receding; this has been coming forward. See the mighty ploughshare and its furrow!"

For the icy mass was heaving up the ground clear across its front, and, on the side where we stood, had evidently found a softer stratum under a forest-covered hill, and inserted its shovel point under the hill, heaved it upon the ice, cracking the rocks into a thousand fragments; and was carrying the whole hill upon its back towards the sea. The large trees were leaning at all angles, some of them submerged, splintered and ground by the crystal torrent, some of the shattered trunks sticking out of the ice. It was one of the most tremendous examples of glacial power I have ever seen.

"I must climb this glacier to-morrow," said Muir. "I shall have a great day of it; I wish you could come along."

I sighed, not with resignation, but with a grief that was akin to despair. The condition of my shoulders was such that it would be madness to attempt to join Muir on his longer and more perilous climbs. I should only spoil his day and endanger his life as well as my own.

That night I baked a good batch of camp bread, boiled a fresh kettle of beans and roasted a leg of venison ready for Muir's breakfast, fixed the coffee-pot and prepared dry kindling for the fire. I knew he would be up and off at daybreak, perhaps long before.

"Wake me up," I admonished him, "or at least take time to make hot coffee before you start." For the wind was rising and the rain pouring, and I knew how imperative the call of such a morning as was promised would be to him. To traverse a great, new, living, rapidly moving glacier would be high joy; but to have a tremendous storm added to this would simply drive Muir wild with desire to be himself a part of the great drama played on the glacier-stage.

Several times during the night I was awakened by the flapping of the tent, the shrieking of the wind in the spruce-tops and the thundering of the ocean surf on the outer barrier of rocks. The tremulous howling of a persistent wolf across the bay soothed me to sleep again, and I did not wake when Muir arose. As I had feared, he was in too big a hurry to take time for breakfast, but pocketed a small cake of camp bread and hastened out into the storm-swept woods. I was aroused, however, by the controversy between him and Stickeen outside of the tent. The little dog, who always slept with one eye and ear alert for Muir's movements, had, as usual, quietly left his warm nest and followed his adopted master. Muir was scolding and expostulating with him as if he were a boy. I chuckled to myself at the futility of Muir's efforts; Stickeen would now, as always, do just as he pleased--and he would please to go along.

Although I was forced to stay at the camp, this stormy day was a most interesting one to me. There was an old Hoonah chief camped at the mouth of the little river which flowed from under Taylor Glacier. He had with him his three wives and a little company of children and grandchildren. The many salmon weirs and summer houses at this point showed that it had been at one time a very important fishing place.

But the advancing glacier had played havoc with the chief's salmon stream. The icy mass had been for several years traveling towards the sea at the rate of at least a mile every year. There were still silver hordes of fine red salmon swimming in the sea outside of the river's mouth. But the stream was now so short that the most of these salmon swam a little ways into the mouth of the river and then out into the salt water again, bewildered and circling about, doubtless wondering what had become of their parent stream.

The old chief came to our camp early, followed by his squaws bearing gifts of salmon, porpoise meat, clams and crabs; and at his command two of the girls of his family picked me a basketful of delicious wild strawberries. He sat motionless by my fire all the forenoon, smoking my leaf tobacco and pondering deeply. After the noon meal, which I shared with him, he called Billy, my interpreter, and asked for a big talk.

With all ceremony I made preparations, gave more presents of leaf tobacco and hardtack and composed myself for the palaver. After the usual preliminaries, in which he told me at great length what a great man I was, how like a father to all the people, comparing me to sun, moon, stars and all other great things; I broke in upon his stream of compliments and asked what he wanted.

Recalled to earth he said: "I wish you to pray to your God."

"For what do you wish me to pray?" I asked.

The old man raised his blanketed form to its full height and waved his hand with a magnificent gesture towards the glacier. "Do you see that great ice mountain?"

"Yes."

"Once," he said, "I had the finest salmon stream upon the coast." Pointing to a point of rock five or six miles beyond the mouth of the glacier he continued: "Once the salmon stream extended far beyond that point of rock. There was a great fall there and a deep pool below it, and here for years great schools of king salmon came crowding up to the foot of that fall. To spear them or net them was very easy; they were the fattest and best salmon among all these islands. My household had abundance of meat for the winter's need. But the cruel spirit of that glacier grew angry with me, I know not why, and drove the ice mountain down towards the sea and spoiled my salmon stream. A year or two more and it will be blotted out entirely. I have done my best. I have prayed to my gods. Last spring I sacrificed two of my slaves, members of my household, my best slaves, a strong man and his wife, to the spirit of that glacier to make the ice mountain stop; but it comes on, and now I want you to pray to *your* God, the God of the white man, to see if He will make the glacier stop!"

I wish I could describe the pathetic earnestness of this old Indian, the simplicity with which he told of the sacrifice of his slaves and the eager look with which he awaited my answer. When I exclaimed in horror at his deed of blood he was astonished; he could not understand.

"Why, they were *my* slaves," he said, "and the man suggested it himself. He was glad to go to death to help his chief."

A few years after this our missionary at Hoonah had the pleasure of baptizing this old chief into the Christian faith. He had put away his slaves and his plural wives, had surrendered the implements of his old superstition, and as a child embraced the new gospel of peace and love. He could not get rid of his superstition about the glacier, however, and about eight years afterwards, visiting at Wrangell, he told me as an item of news which he expected would greatly please me that, doubtless as a result of my prayers, Taylor Glacier was receding again and the salmon beginning to come into that stream.

At intervals during this eventful day I went to the face of the glacier and even climbed the disintegrating hill that was riding on the glacier's ploughshare, in an effort to see the bold wanderers; but the jagged ice peaks of the high glacial rapids blocked my vision, and the rain driving passionately in horizontal sheets shut out the mountains and the upper plateau of ice. I could see that it was snowing on the glacier, and imagined the weariness and peril of dog and man exposed to the storm in that dangerous region. I could only hope that Muir had not ventured to face the wind on the glacier, but had contented himself with tracing its eastern side, and was somewhere in the woods bordering it, beside a big fire, studying storm and glacier in comparative safety.

When the shadows of evening were added to those of the storm I had my men gather materials for a big bonfire, and kindle it well out on the flat, where it could be seen from mountain and glacier. I placed dry clothing and blankets in the fly tent facing the camp-fire, and got ready the best supper at my command: clam chowder, fried porpoise, bacon and beans, "savory meat" made of mountain kid with potatoes, onions, rice and curry, camp biscuit and coffee, with dessert of wild strawberries and condensed milk.

It grew pitch-dark before seven, and it was after ten when the dear wanderers staggered into camp out of the dripping forest. Stickeen did not bounce in ahead with a bark, as was his custom, but crept silently to his piece of blanket and curled down, too tired to shake himself. Billy and I laid hands on Muir without a word, and in a trice he was stripped of his wet garments, rubbed dry, clothed in dry underwear, wrapped in a blanket and set down on a bed of spruce twigs with a plate of hot chowder before him. When the chowder disappeared the other hot dishes followed in quick succession, without a question asked or a word uttered. Lot kept the fire blazing just right, Joe kept the victuals hot and baked fresh bread, while Billy and I waited on Muir.

Not till he came to the coffee and strawberries did Muir break the silence. "Yon's a brave doggie," he said. Stickeen, who could not yet be induced to eat, responded by a glance of one eye and a feeble pounding of the blanket with his heavy tail.

Then Muir began to talk, and little by little, between sips of coffee, the story of the day was unfolded. Soon memories crowded for utterance and I listened till midnight, entranced by a succession of vivid descriptions the like of which I have never heard before or since. The fierce music and grandeur of the storm, the expanse of ice with its bewildering crevasses, its mysterious contortions, its solemn voices were made to live before me.

[Illustration: GLACIAL CREVASSES

"We had to make long, narrow tacks and doublings, tracing the edges of tremendous transverse and longitudinal crevasses--beautiful and awful"]

When Muir described his marooning on the narrow island of ice surrounded by fathomless crevasses, with a knife-edged sliver curving deeply "like the cable of a suspension bridge" diagonally across it as the only means of escape, I shuddered at his peril. I held my breath as he told of the terrible risks he ran as he cut his steps down the wall of ice to the bridge's end, knocked off the sharp edge of the sliver, hitched across inch by inch and climbed the still more difficult ascent on the other side. But when he told of Stickeen's cries of despair at being left on the other side of the crevasse, of his heroic determination at last to do or die, of his careful progress across the sliver as he braced himself against the gusts and dug his little claws into the ice, and of his passionate revulsion to the heights of exultation when, intoxicated by his escape, he became a living whirlwind of joy, flashing about in mad gyrations, shouting and screaming "Saved! saved!" my tears streamed down my face. Before the close of the story Stickeen arose, stepped slowly across to Muir and crouched down with his head on Muir's foot, gazing into his face and murmuring soft canine words of adoration to his god.

Not until 1897, seventeen years after the event, did Muir give to the public his story of Stickeen. How many times he had written and rewritten it I know not. He told me at the time of its first publication that he had been thinking of the story all of these years and jotting down paragraphs and sentences as they occurred to him. He was never satisfied with a sentence until it balanced well. He had the keenest sense of melody, as well as of harmony, in his sentence structure, and this great dog-story of his is a remarkable instance of the growth to perfection of the great production of a great master.

The wonderful power of endurance of this man, whom Theodore Roosevelt has well called a "perfectly natural man," is instanced by the fact that, although he was gone about seventeen hours on this day of his adventure with Stickeen, with only a bite of bread to eat, and never rested a minute of that time, but was battling with the storm all day and often racing at full speed across the glacier, yet he got up at daylight the next morning, breakfasted with me and was gone all day again, with Stickeen at his heels, climbing a high mountain to get a view of the snow fountains and upper reaches of the glacier; and when he returned after nightfall he worked for two or three hours at his notes and sketches.

The latter part of this voyage was hurried. Muir had a wife waiting for him at home and he had promised to stay in Alaska only one month. He had dallied so long with his icy loves, the glaciers, that we were obliged to make all haste to Sitka, where he expected to take the return steamer. To miss that would condemn him to Alaska and absence from his wife for another month. Through a continually pouring rain we sailed by the then deserted town of Hoonah, ascended with the rising tide a long, narrow, shallow inlet, dragged our canoe a hundred yards over a little hill and then descended with the receding tide another long, narrow passage down to Chatham Strait; and so on to the mouth of Peril Strait which divided Baranof from Chichagof Island.

On the other side of Chatham Strait, opposite the mouth of Peril, we visited again Angoon, the village of the Hootz-noos. From this town the painted and drunken warriors had come the winter before and attacked the Stickeens, killing old Tow-a-att, Moses and another of our Christian Indians. The trouble was not settled yet, and although the two tribes had exchanged some pledges and promised to fight no more, I feared a fresh outbreak, and so thought it wise to pay another visit to the Hootz-noos. As we approached Angoon, however, I heard the war-drums beating with their peculiar cadence, "tum-tum"--a beat off--"tum-tum, tum-tum." As we came up to the beach I saw what was seemingly the whole tribe dancing their war-dances, arrayed in their war-paint with their fantastic war-gear on. So earnestly engaged were they in their dance that they at first paid no attention whatever to me. My heart sank into my boots. "They are going back to Wrangell to attack the Stickeens," I thought, "and there will be another bloody war."

Driving our canoe ashore, we hurried up to the head chief of the Hootz-noos, who was alternately haranguing his people and directing the dances.

"Anatlask," I called, "what does this mean? You are going on the warpath. Tell me what you are about. Are you going back to Stickeen?"

He looked at me vacantly a little while, and then a grin spread from ear to ear. It was the same chief in whose house I had seen the idiot boy a year before.

"Come with me," he said.

He led us into his house and across the room to where in state, surrounded by all kinds of chieftain's gear, Chilcat blankets, totemic carvings and paintings, chieftain's hats and cunningly woven baskets, there lay the body of a stalwart young man wrapped in a button-embroidered blanket. The chief silently removed the blanket from the face of the dead. The skull was completely crushed on one side as by a heavy blow. Then the story came out.

The hootz, or big brown bear of that country, is as large and savage as the grizzly bear of the Rockies. At certain seasons he is, as the natives say, "quonsum-sollex" (always mad). The natives seldom attack these bears, confining their attention to the more timid and easily killed black bears. But this young man with a companion, hunting on Baranof Island across the Strait, found himself suddenly confronted by an enormous hootz. The young man rashly shot him with his musket, wounding him sufficiently to make him furious. The tremendous brute hurled his thousand pounds of ferocity at the hunter, and one little tap of that huge paw crushed his skull like an egg-shell. His companion brought his body home; and now the whole tribe had formally declared war on that bear, and all this dancing and painting and drumming was in preparation for a war party, composed of all the men, dogs and guns in the town. They were going on the warpath to get that bear. Greatly relieved, I gave them my blessing and sped them on their way.

We had been rowing all night before this incident, and all the next night we sailed up the tortuous Peril Strait, going upward with the flood, one man steering while the other slept, to the meeting place of the waters; then down with the receding tide through the islands, and so on to Sitka. Here we met a warm reception from the missionaries, and also from the captain and officers of the old man-of-war *Jamestown*, afterwards used as a school ship for the navy in the harbor of San Francisco.

Alaska at that time had no vestige of civil government, no means of punishing crime, no civil officers except the customs collectors, no magistrate or police,--everyone was a law to himself. The only sign of authority was this cumbersome sailing vessel with its marines and sailors. It could not move out of Sitka harbor without first sending by the monthly mail steamer to San Francisco for a tug to come and tow it through these intricate channels to the sea where the sails could be spread. Of course, it was not of much use to this vast territory. The officers of the *Jamestown* were supposed to be doing some surveying, but, lacking the means of travel, what they did amounted to very little.

They were interested at once in our account of the discovery of Glacier Bay and of the other unmapped bays and inlets that we had entered. At their request, from Muir's notes and our estimate of distances by our rate of sailing, and of directions from observations of our little compass, we drew a rough map of Glacier Bay. This was sent on to Washington by these officers and published by the Navy Department. For six or seven years it was the only sailing chart of Glacier Bay, and two or three steamers were wrecked, groping their way in these uncharted passages, before surveying vessels began to make accurate maps. So from its beginning has Uncle Sam neglected this greatest and richest of all his possessions.

Our little company separated at Sitka. Stickeen and our Indian crew were the first to leave, embarking for a return trip to Wrangell by canoe. Stickeen had stuck close to Muir, following him everywhere, crouching at his feet where he sat, sleeping in his room at night. When the time came for him to leave Muir explained the matter to him fully, talking to and reasoning with him as if he were human. Billy led him aboard the canoe by a dog-chain, and the last Muir saw of him he was standing on of the canoe, howling a sad farewell.

Muir sailed south on the monthly mail steamer; while I took passage on a trading steamer for another missionary trip among the northern tribes.

So ended my canoe voyages with John Muir. Their memory is fresh and sweet as ever. The flowing stream of years has not washed away nor dimmed the impressions of those great days we spent together. Nearly all of them were cold, wet and uncomfortable, if one were merely an animal, to be depressed or enlivened by physical conditions. But of these so-called "hardships" Muir made nothing, and I caught his spirit; therefore, the beauty, the glory, the wonder and the thrills of those weeks of exploration are with me yet and shall endure--a rustless, inexhaustible treasure.

THE MAN IN PERSPECTIVE

JOHN MUIR

He lived aloft, exultant, unafraid. All things were good to him. The mountain old Stretched gnarled hands to help him climb. The peak Waved blithe snow-banner greeting; and for him The rav'ning storm, aprowl for human life, Purred like the lion at his trainer's feet. The grizzly met him on the narrow ledge, Gave gruff "good morning"--and the right of way. The blue-veined glacier, cold of heart and pale, Warmed, at his gaze, to amethystine blush, And murmured deep, fond undertones of love.

He walked apart from men, yet loved his kind, And brought them treasures from his larger store. For them he delved in mines of richer gold. Earth's messenger he was to human hearts. The starry moss flower from its dizzy shelf, The ouzel, shaking forth its spray of song, The glacial runlet, tinkling its clear bell, The rose-of-morn, abloom on snowy heights-- Each sent by him a jewel-word of cheer. Blind eyes he opened and deaf ears unstopped.

He lived aloft, apart. He talked with God In all the myriad tongues of God's sweet world; But still he came anear and talked with us, Interpreting for God to listn'ing men.

[Illustration: JOHN MUIR IN LATER LIFE]

VII

THE MAN IN PERSPECTIVE

The friendship between John Muir and myself was of that fine sort which grows and deepens with absence almost as well as with companionship. Occasional letters passed from one to the other. When I felt like writing to Muir I obeyed the impulse without asking whether I "owed" him a letter, and he followed the same rule--or rather lack of rule. Sometimes answers to these letters came quickly; sometimes they were long delayed, so long that they were not answers at all. When I sent him "news of his mountains and glaciers" that contained items really novel to him his replies were immediate and enthusiastic. When he had found in his great outdoor museum some peculiar treasure he talked over his find with me by letter.

Muir's letters were never commonplace and sometimes they were long and rich. I preserved them all; and when, a few years ago, an Alaska steamboat sank to the bottom of the Yukon, carrying with it my library and all my literary possessions, the loss of these letters from my friend caused me more sorrow than the loss of almost any other of my many priceless treasures.

The summer of 1881, the year following that of our second canoe voyage, Muir went, as scientific and literary expert, with the U.S. revenue cutter *Rogers*, which was sent by the Government into the Arctic Ocean in search of the ill-fated De Long exploring party. His published articles written on the revenue cutter were of great interest; but in his more intimate letters to me there was a note of disappointment.

"There have been no mountains to climb," he wrote, "although I have had entrancing long-distance views of many. I have not had a chance to visit any glaciers. There were no trees in those arctic regions, and but few flowers. Of God's process of modeling the world I saw but little--nothing for days but that limitless, relentless ice-pack. I was confined within the narrow prison of the ship; I had no freedom, I went at the will of other men; not of my own. It was very different from those glorious canoe voyages with you in your beautiful, fruitful wilderness."

A very brief visit at Muir's home near Martinez, California, in the spring of 1883 found him at what he frankly said was very distasteful work--managing a large fruit ranch. He was doing the work well and making his orchards pay large dividends; but his heart was in the hills and woods. Eagerly he questioned me of my travels and of the "progress" of the glaciers and woods of Alaska. Beyond a few short mountain trips he had seen nothing for two years of his beloved wilds.

Passionately he voiced his discontent: "I am losing the precious days. I am degenerating into a machine for making money. I am learning nothing in this trivial world of men. I must break away and get out into the mountains to learn the news."

In 1888 the ten years' limit which I had set for service in Alaska expired. The educational necessities of my children and the feeling that was growing upon me like a smothering cloud that if I remained much longer among the Indians I would lose all power to talk or write good English, drove me from the Northwest to find a temporary home in Southern California.

I had not notified Muir of my coming, but suddenly appeared in his orchard at Martinez one day in early summer. It was cherry-picking time and he was out among his trees superintending a large force of workmen. He saw me as soon as I discovered him, and dropping the basket he was carrying came running to greet me with both hands outstretched.

"Ah! my friend," he cried, "I have been longing mightily for you. You have come to take me on a canoe trip to the countries beyond--to Lituya and Yakutat bays and Prince William Sound; have you not? My weariness of this hum-drum, work-a-day life has grown so heavy it is like to crush me. I'm ready to break away and go with you whenever you say."

"No," I replied, "I am leaving Alaska."

"Man, man!" protested Muir, "how can you do it? You'll never carry out such a notion as that in the world. Your heart will cry every day for the North like a lost child; and in your sleep the snow-banners of your white peaks will beckon to you.

"Why, look at me," he said, "and take warning. I'm a horrible example. I, who have breathed the mountain air--who have really lived a life of freedom--condemned to penal servitude with these miserable little bald-heads!" (holding up a bunch of cherries). "Boxing them up; putting them in prison! And for money! Man! I'm like to die of the shame of it.

"And then you're not safe a day in this sordid world of money-grubbing men. I came near dying a mean, civilized death, the other day. A Chinaman emptied a bucket of phosphorus over me and almost burned me up. How different that would have been from a nice white death in the crevasse of a glacier!

"Gin it were na for my bairnies I'd rin awa' frae a' this tribble an' hale ye back north wi' me."

So Muir would run on, now in English, now in broad Scotch; but through all his raillery there ran a note of longing for the wilderness. "I want to see what is going on," he said. "So many great events are happening, and I'm not there to see them. I'm learning nothing here that will do me any good."

I spent the night with him, and we talked till long after midnight, sailing anew our voyages of enchantment. He had just completed his work of editing "Picturesque California" and gave me a set of the beautiful volumes.

Our paths did not converge again for nine years; but I was to have, after all, a few more Alaska days with John Muir. The itch of the wanderlust in my feet had become a wearisome, nervous ache, increasing with the years, and the call of the wild more imperative, until the fierce yearning for the North was at times more than I could bear.

The first of the great northward gold stampedes--that of 1897 to the Klondyke in Northwestern Canada on the borders of Alaska--afforded me the opportunity for which I was longing to return to the land of my heart. The latter part of August saw me on *The Queen*, the largest of that great fleet of passenger boats that were traversing the thousand miles of wonder and beauty between Seattle and Skagway. These steamboats were all laden with gold seekers and their goods. Seattle sprang into prominence and wealth, doubling her population in a few months. From every community in the United States, from all Canada and from many lands across the oceans came that strange mob of lawyers, doctors, clerks, merchants, farmers, mechanics, engineers, reporters, sharpers--all gold-struck--all mad with excitement--all rushing pell-mell into a thousand new and hard experiences.

As I stood on the upper deck of the vessel, watching the strange scene on the dock, who should come up the gang-plank but John Muir, wearing the same old gray ulster and Scotch cap! It was the last place in the world I would have looked for him. But he was not stampeding to the Klondyke. His being there at that time was really an accident. In company with two other eminent "tree-men" he had been spending the summer in the study of the forests of Canada and the three were "climaxing," as they said, in the forests of Alaska.

Five pleasurable days we had together on board *The Queen*. Muir was vastly amused by the motley crowd of excited men, their various outfits, their queer equipment, their ridiculous notions of camping and life in the wilderness. "A nest of ants," he called them, "taken to a strange country and stirred up with a stick."

As our steamboat touched at Port Townsend, Muir received a long telegram from a San Francisco newspaper, offering him a large sum if he would go over the mountains and down the Yukon to the Klondyke, and write them letters about conditions there. He brought the telegram to me, laughing heartily at the absurdity of anybody making him such a proposition.

"Do they think I'm daft," he asked, "like a' the lave o' thae puir bodies? When I go into that wild it will not be in a crowd like this or on such a sordid mission. Ah! my old friend, they'll be spoiling our grand Alaska."

He offered to secure for me the reporter's job tendered to him. I refused, urging my lack of training for such work and my more important and responsible position.

"Why, that same paper has a host of reporters on the way to the Klondyke now," I said. "There is ----" (naming a noted poet and author of the Coast). "He must be half-way down to Dawson by this time."

"---- doesn't count," replied Muir, "for the patent reason that everybody knows he can't tell the truth. The poor fellow is not to blame for it. He was just made that way. Everybody will read with delight his wonderful tales of the trail, but nobody will believe him. We all know him too well."

Muir contracted a hard cold the first night out from Seattle. The hot, close stateroom and a cold blast through the narrow window were the cause. A distressing cough racked his whole frame. When he refused to go to a physician who was on the boat I brought the doctor to him. After the usual examination the physician asked, "What do you generally do for a cold?"

"Oh," said Muir, "I shiver it away."

"Explain yourself," said the puzzled doctor.

"We-ll," drawled Muir, "two or three years ago I camped by the Muir Glacier for a week. I had caught just such a cold as this from the same cause--a stuffy stateroom. So I made me a little sled out of spruce boughs, put a blanket and some sea biscuit on it and set out up the glacier. I got into a labyrinth of crevasses and a driving snowstorm, and had to spend the night on the ice ten miles from land. I sat on the sled all night or thrashed about it, and had a dickens of a time; I shivered so hard I shook the sled to pieces. When morning came my cold was all gone. That is my prescription, Doctor. You are welcome to use it in your practice."

"Well," laughed the doctor, "if I had such patients as you in such a country as this I might try your heroic remedy, but I am afraid it would hardly serve in general practice."

Muir and I made the most of these few days together, and walked the decks till late each night, for he had much to tell me. He had at last written his story of Stickeen; and was working on books treating of the Big Trees, the National Parks and the glaciers of Alaska.

At Wrangell, as we went ashore, we were greeted by joyful exclamations from the little company of old Stickeen Indians we found on the dock. That sharp intaking of the breath which is the Thlinget's note of surprise and delight, and the words *Nuknate Ankow ka Glate Ankow* (Priest Chief and Ice Chief) passed along the line. Death had made many gaps in the old circle of friends, both white and native, but the welcome from those who remained warmed our hearts.

From Wrangell northward the steamboat followed the route of our canoe voyage of 1880 through Wrangell Narrows into Prince Frederick Sound, past Norris Glacier and Holkham Bay into Stevens Passage, past Taku Bay to Juneau and on to Lynn Canal--then on the track of our voyage of 1879 up to Haines and beyond fifteen miles to that new, chaotic camp in the woods called Skagway.

The two or three days which it took *The Queen* to discharge her load of passengers and cargo of their outfits were spent by Muir and his scientific companions in roaming the forests and mountains about Skagway and examining the flora of that region. They kept mostly off the trail of the struggling, straggling army of *Cheechakoes* (newcomers) who were blunderingly trying to get their goods and themselves across the rugged, jagged mountains on their way to the promised land of gold; but Muir found time to spend some hours with me in my camp under a hemlock, where he ate again of my cooking over a camp-fire.

"You are going on a strange journey this time, my friend," he admonished me. "I don't envy you. You'll have a hard time keeping your heart light and simple in the midst of this crowd of madmen. Instead of the music of the wind among the spruce-tops and the tinkling of the waterfalls, your ears will be filled with the oaths and groans of these poor, deluded, self-burdened men. Keep close to Nature's heart, yourself; and break clear away, once in a while, and climb a mountain or spend a week in the woods. Wash your spirit clean from the earth-stains of this sordid, gold-seeking crowd in God's pure air. It will help you in your efforts to bring to these men something better than gold. Don't lose your freedom and your love of the Earth as God made it."

In 1899 it was my good fortune to have one more Alaska day with John Muir at Skagway. After a year in the Klondyke I had spent the winter of 1898-99 in the Eastern States arousing the Christian public to the needs of this newly discovered Empire of the North; and was returning with other ministers to interior and western Alaska. The White Pass Railroad was completed only to the summit; and it was a laborious task, requiring a month of very hard work, to get our goods from Skagway over the thirty miles of mountains to Lake Bennett, where we could load them on our open boat for the voyage of two thousand miles down the Yukon.

While I was engaged in this task there came to Skagway the steamship *George W. Elder*, carrying one of the most remarkable companies of scientific men ever gathered together in one expedition. Mr. Harriman, the great railroad magnate, had chartered the steamer, and had invited as his guests many men of world reputation in various branches of natural science. Among them were John Burroughs, Drs. Merriam and Dahl of the Smithsonian Institute, and, not least, John Muir. Indeed he was called the Nestor of the expedition and his advice followed as that of no other.

The enticing proposition was made me by Muir, and backed by Mr. Harriman's personal invitation, that I should join this distinguished company, share Muir's stateroom and spend the summer cruising along the southern and western coasts of Alaska. However, the new mining camps were calling with a still more imperative voice, and I had to turn my back to the Coast and face the great, sun-bathed Interior. But what a joy and inspiration it would have been to climb Muir, Geicke and Taylor glaciers again with Muir, note the rapid progress God was making in His work of landscape gardening by means of these great tools, make at last our deferred visits to Lituya and Yakutat bays and the fine glaciers of Prince William's Sound, and renew my studies of this good world under my great Master.

A letter from Muir about his summer's cruise, written in November, 1899, reached me at Nome in June, 1900; for those of us who had reached that bleak, exposed northwestern coast and wintered there did not get any mail for six months. We were fifteen hundred miles from a post-office.

In his letter Muir wrote: "The voyage was a grand one, and I saw much that was new to me and packed full of interest and instruction. But, do you know, I longed to break away from the steamboat and its splendid company, get a dugout canoe and a crew of Indians, and, with you as my companion, poke into the nooks and crannies of the mountains and glaciers which we could not reach from the steamer. What great days we have had together, you and I!"

This day at Skagway, in 1899, was the last of my Alaska days with John Muir, except as I bring them back and live them over in my thoughts. How often in my long voyages, by canoe or steamer, among the thousand islands of southeastern Alaska, the intricate channels of Prince William's Sound, the great rivers, and multitudinous lakes of the Interior, and the treeless, windswept coasts of Bering Sea and the Arctic Ocean; or in my tramps in the summer over the mountains and plains of Alaska, or in the winter with my dogs over the frozen wilderness fighting the great battle with the fierce cold or spellbound under the magic of the Aurora--how often have I longed for the presence of Muir to heighten my enjoyment by his higher ecstasy, or reveal to me what I was too dull to see or understand. I have had inspiring companions, and my life has been blessed by many friendships inestimably precious and rich; but for me the World has produced but one John Muir; and to no other man do I feel that I owe so much; for I was blind and he made me see!

Only once since 1899 did I meet him, and then but for an hour at his temporary home in Los Angeles in 1910. He was putting the finishing touches on his rich volume, "The Story of My Boyhood and Youth." I submitted for his review and correction the article which forms the first two chapters of this book. With that nice regard for absolute verity which always characterized him he pointed out two or three passages in which his recollection clashed with mine, and I at once made the changes he suggested.

Muir never grew old. After he was sixty years of age (as men count age) some of his most daring feats of mountain climbing and some of his longest journeys into the wilds were undertaken. When he was past seventy he was still tramping and camping in the forests and among the hills. When he was seventy-three he made long trips to South America and Africa, and to the very end he was exploring, studying, working and enjoying.

All his writings exult with the spirit of immortal youth. There is in his books an intimate companionship with the trees, the mountains, the flowers and the animals, that is altogether fine. Surely no such books of mountains and forests were ever written as his "Mountains of California," "My First Summer in the Sierra," "The Yosemite" and "Our National Parks." His brooks and trees are the abode of dryads and hamadryads--they live and talk.

And when he writes of the animals he has met in his rambles, without any attempt to put into their characters anything that does not belong to them, without "manufacturing his data," he somehow manages to do much more than introduce them to you; he makes you their intimate and admiring friends, as he was. His ouzel bobs you a cheery good morning and sprays you with its "ripple of song"; his Douglas squirrel scolds and swears at you with rough good-nature; and his big-horn gazes at you with frank and friendly eyes and challenges you to follow to its splendid heights, not as a hunter but as a companion. You love them all, as Muir did.

As an instance of this power in his writings, when I returned from the Klondyke in 1898 the story of Stickeen had been published in a magazine a few months before. I met in New York a daughter of the great Field family, who when a child had heard me tell of Muir's exploit in rescuing me from the mountain top, and who had shouted with delight when I told of our sliding down the mountain in the moraine gravel. She asked me eagerly if I was the Mr. Young mentioned in Muir's story. When I said that I was she called to her companions and introduced me as the Owner of Stickeen; and I was content to have as my claim to an earthly immortality my ownership of an immortalized dog.

I cannot think of John Muir as dead, or as much changed from the man with whom I canoed and camped. He was too much a part of nature--too natural--to be separated from his mountains, trees and glaciers. Somewhere, I am sure, he is making other explorations, solving other natural problems, using that brilliant, inventive genius to good effect; and some time again I shall hear him unfold anew, with still clearer insight and more eloquent words, fresh secrets of his "mountains of God."

The Thlingets have a Happy Hunting Ground in the Spirit Land for dogs as well as for men; and Muir used to contend that they were right--that the so-called lower animals have as much right to a Heaven as humans. I wonder if he has found a still more beautiful--a glorified--Stickeen; and if the little fellow still follows and frisks about him as in those old days. I like to think so; and when I too cross the Great Divide--and it can't be long now--I shall look eagerly for them both to be my companions in fresh adventures. In the meantime I am lonely for them and think of them often, and say, with *The Harvester*, "What a dog!--and what a MAN!!"

PRINTED IN THE UNITED STATES OF AMERICA

---

* * * * * *

Transcriberís note:

The punctuation and spelling from the original text have been faithfully preserved.

END OF THE PROJECT GUTENBERG EBOOK ALASKA DAYS WITH JOHN MUIR

******* This file should be named 30697-8.txt or 30697-8.zip
****

This and all associated files of various formats will be found in:
http://www.gutenberg.org/dirs/3/0/6/9/30697

Updated editions will replace the previous one--the old editions will be renamed.

Creating the works from public domain print editions means that no one owns a United States copyright in these works, so the Foundation (and you!) can copy and distribute it in the United States without permission and without paying copyright royalties. Special rules, set forth in the General Terms of Use part of this license, apply to copying and distributing Project Gutenberg-tm electronic works to protect the PROJECT GUTENBERG-tm concept and trademark. Project Gutenberg is a registered trademark, and may not be used if you charge for the eBooks, unless you receive specific permission. If you do not charge anything for copies of this eBook, complying with the rules is very easy. You may use this eBook for nearly any purpose such as creation of derivative works, reports, performances and research. They may be modified and printed and given away--you may do practically ANYTHING with public domain eBooks. Redistribution is subject to the trademark license, especially commercial redistribution.

Section 1. General Terms of Use and Redistributing Project Gutenberg-tm electronic works

1.A. By reading or using any part of this Project Gutenberg-tm electronic work, you indicate that you have read, understand, agree to and accept all the terms of this license and intellectual property (trademark/copyright) agreement. If you do not agree to abide by all the terms of this agreement, you must cease using and return or destroy all copies of Project Gutenberg-tm electronic works in your possession. If you paid a fee for obtaining a copy of or access to a Project Gutenberg-tm electronic work and you do not agree to be bound by the terms of this agreement, you may obtain a refund from the person or entity to whom you paid the fee as set forth in paragraph 1.E.8.

1.B. "Project Gutenberg" is a registered trademark. It may only be used on or associated in any way with an electronic work by people who agree to be bound by the terms of this agreement. There are a few things that you can do with most Project Gutenberg-tm electronic works even without complying with the full terms of this agreement. See paragraph 1.C below. There are a lot of things you can do with Project Gutenberg-tm electronic works if you follow the terms of this agreement and help preserve free future access to Project Gutenberg-tm electronic works. See paragraph 1.E below.

1.C. The Project Gutenberg Literary Archive Foundation ("the Foundation" or PGLAF), owns a compilation copyright in the collection of Project Gutenberg-tm electronic works. Nearly all the individual works in the collection are in the public domain in the United States. If an individual work is in the public domain in the United States and you are located in the United States, we do not claim a right to prevent you from copying, distributing, performing, displaying or creating derivative works based on the work as long as all references to Project Gutenberg are removed. Of course, we hope that you will support the Project

Gutenberg-tm mission of promoting free access to electronic works by freely sharing Project Gutenberg-tm works in compliance with the terms of this agreement for keeping the Project Gutenberg-tm name associated with the work. You can easily comply with the terms of this agreement by keeping this work in the same format with its attached full Project Gutenberg-tm License when you share it without charge with others.

1.D. The copyright laws of the place where you are located also govern what you can do with this work. Copyright laws in most countries are in a constant state of change. If you are outside the United States, check the laws of your country in addition to the terms of this agreement before downloading, copying, displaying, performing, distributing or creating derivative works based on this work or any other Project Gutenberg-tm work. The Foundation makes no representations concerning the copyright status of any work in any country outside the United States.

1.E. Unless you have removed all references to Project Gutenberg:

1.E.1. The following sentence, with active links to, or other immediate access to, the full Project Gutenberg-tm License must appear prominently whenever any copy of a Project Gutenberg-tm work (any work on which the phrase "Project Gutenberg" appears, or with which the phrase "Project Gutenberg" is associated) is accessed, displayed, performed, viewed, copied or distributed:

This eBook is for the use of anyone anywhere at no cost and with almost no restrictions whatsoever. You may copy it, give it away or re-use it under the terms of the Project Gutenberg License included with this eBook or online at www.gutenberg.org

used in the official version posted on the official Project
Gutenberg-tm web site (www.gutenberg.org), you must, at no
additional cost, fee or expense to the user, provide a copy, a
means of exporting a copy, or a means of obtaining a copy upon
request, of the work in its original "Plain Vanilla ASCII" or other
form. Any alternate format must include the full Project
Gutenberg-tm License as specified in paragraph 1.E.1.

1.E.7. Do not charge a fee for access to, viewing, displaying,
performing, copying or distributing any Project Gutenberg-tm
works unless you comply with paragraph 1.E.8 or 1.E.9.

1.E.8. You may charge a reasonable fee for copies of or
providing access to or distributing Project Gutenberg-tm
electronic works provided that

- You pay a royalty fee of 20% of the gross profits you derive
from the use of Project Gutenberg-tm works calculated using the
method you already use to calculate your applicable taxes. The
fee is owed to the owner of the Project Gutenberg-tm trademark,
but he has agreed to donate royalties under this paragraph to the
Project Gutenberg Literary Archive Foundation. Royalty
payments must be paid within 60 days following each date on
which you prepare (or are legally required to prepare) your
periodic tax returns. Royalty payments should be clearly marked
as such and sent to the Project Gutenberg Literary Archive
Foundation at the address specified in Section 4, "Information
about donations to the Project Gutenberg Literary Archive
Foundation."

- You provide a full refund of any money paid by a user who
notifies you in writing (or by e-mail) within 30 days of receipt that
s/he does not agree to the terms of the full Project Gutenberg-tm
License. You must require such a user to return or destroy all
copies of the works possessed in a physical medium and
discontinue all use of and all access to other copies of Project

Gutenberg-tm works.

- You provide, in accordance with paragraph 1.F.3, a full refund of any money paid for a work or a replacement copy, if a defect in the electronic work is discovered and reported to you within 90 days of receipt of the work.

- You comply with all other terms of this agreement for free distribution of Project Gutenberg-tm works.

1.E.9. If you wish to charge a fee or distribute a Project Gutenberg-tm electronic work or group of works on different terms than are set forth in this agreement, you must obtain permission in writing from both the Project Gutenberg Literary Archive Foundation and Michael Hart, the owner of the Project Gutenberg-tm trademark. Contact the Foundation as set forth in Section 3 below.

1.F.

1.F.1. Project Gutenberg volunteers and employees expend considerable effort to identify, do copyright research on, transcribe and proofread public domain works in creating the Project Gutenberg-tm collection. Despite these efforts, Project Gutenberg-tm electronic works, and the medium on which they may be stored, may contain "Defects," such as, but not limited to, incomplete, inaccurate or corrupt data, transcription errors, a copyright or other intellectual property infringement, a defective or damaged disk or other medium, a computer virus, or computer codes that damage or cannot be read by your equipment.

1.F.2. LIMITED WARRANTY, DISCLAIMER OF DAMAGES - Except for the "Right of Replacement or Refund" described in paragraph 1.F.3, the Project Gutenberg Literary Archive Foundation, the owner of the Project Gutenberg-tm trademark, and any other party distributing a Project Gutenberg-tm electronic work under this agreement, disclaim all liability to you for damages, costs and expenses, including legal fees. YOU AGREE THAT YOU HAVE NO REMEDIES FOR NEGLIGENCE, STRICT LIABILITY, BREACH OF WARRANTY OR BREACH OF CONTRACT EXCEPT THOSE PROVIDED IN PARAGRAPH F3. YOU AGREE THAT THE FOUNDATION, THE TRADEMARK OWNER, AND ANY DISTRIBUTOR UNDER THIS AGREEMENT WILL NOT BE LIABLE TO YOU FOR ACTUAL, DIRECT, INDIRECT, CONSEQUENTIAL, PUNITIVE OR INCIDENTAL DAMAGES EVEN IF YOU GIVE NOTICE OF THE POSSIBILITY OF SUCH DAMAGE.

1.F.3. LIMITED RIGHT OF REPLACEMENT OR REFUND - If you discover a defect in this electronic work within 90 days of receiving it, you can receive a refund of the money (if any) you paid for it by sending a written explanation to the person you received the work from. If you received the work on a physical medium, you must return the medium with your written explanation. The person or entity that provided you with the defective work may elect to provide a replacement copy in lieu of a refund. If you received the work electronically, the person or entity providing it to you may choose to give you a second opportunity to receive the work electronically in lieu of a refund. If the second copy is also defective, you may demand a refund in writing without further opportunities to fix the problem.

1.F.4. Except for the limited right of replacement or refund set forth in paragraph 1.F.3, this work is provided to you 'AS-IS', WITH NO OTHER WARRANTIES OF ANY KIND, EXPRESS OR IMPLIED, INCLUDING BUT NOT LIMITED TO WARRANTIES OF MERCHANTIBILITY OR FITNESS FOR ANY PURPOSE.

1.F.5. Some states do not allow disclaimers of certain implied warranties or the exclusion or limitation of certain types of damages. If any disclaimer or limitation set forth in this agreement violates the law of the state applicable to this agreement, the agreement shall be interpreted to make the maximum disclaimer or limitation permitted by the applicable state law. The invalidity or unenforceability of any provision of this agreement shall not void the remaining provisions.

1.F.6. **INDEMNITY**

- You agree to indemnify and hold the Foundation, the trademark owner, any agent or employee of the Foundation, anyone providing copies of Project Gutenberg-tm electronic works in accordance with this agreement, and any volunteers associated with the production, promotion and distribution of Project Gutenberg-tm electronic works, harmless from all liability, costs and expenses, including legal fees, that arise directly or indirectly from any of the following which you do or cause to occur: (a) distribution of this or any Project Gutenberg-tm work, (b) alteration, modification, or additions or deletions to any Project Gutenberg-tm work, and (c) any Defect you cause.

Section 2. Information about the Mission of Project Gutenberg-tm

Project Gutenberg-tm is synonymous with the free distribution of electronic works in formats readable by the widest variety of computers including obsolete, old, middle-aged and new computers. It exists because of the efforts of hundreds of volunteers and donations from people in all walks of life.

Volunteers and financial support to provide volunteers with the assistance they need are critical to reaching Project Gutenberg-tm's goals and ensuring that the Project Gutenberg-tm collection will remain freely available for generations to come. In 2001, the Project Gutenberg Literary Archive Foundation was created to provide a secure and permanent future for Project Gutenberg-tm and future generations. To learn more about the Project Gutenberg Literary Archive Foundation and how your efforts and donations can help, see Sections 3 and 4 and the Foundation web page at http://www.gutenberg.org/fundraising/pglaf.

Section 3. Information about the Project Gutenberg Literary Archive Foundation

The Project Gutenberg Literary Archive Foundation is a non profit 501(c)(3) educational corporation organized under the laws of the state of Mississippi and granted tax exempt status by the Internal Revenue Service. The Foundation's EIN or federal tax identification number is 64-6221541. Contributions to the Project Gutenberg Literary Archive Foundation are tax deductible to the full extent permitted by U.S. federal laws and your state's laws.

The Foundation's principal office is located at 4557 Melan Dr. S. Fairbanks, AK, 99712., but its volunteers and employees are scattered throughout numerous locations. Its business office is located at 809 North 1500 West, Salt Lake City, UT 84116, (801) 596-1887, email business@pglaf.org. Email contact links and up to date contact information can be found at the Foundation's web site and official page at http://www.gutenberg.org/about/contact

For additional contact information: Dr. Gregory B. Newby Chief Executive and Director gbnewby@pglaf.org

Section 4. Information about Donations to the Project Gutenberg Literary Archive Foundation

Project Gutenberg-tm depends upon and cannot survive without wide spread public support and donations to carry out its mission of increasing the number of public domain and licensed works that can be freely distributed in machine readable form accessible by the widest array of equipment including outdated equipment. Many small donations ($1 to $5,000) are particularly important to maintaining tax exempt status with the IRS.

The Foundation is committed to complying with the laws regulating charities and charitable donations in all 50 states of the United States. Compliance requirements are not uniform and it takes a considerable effort, much paperwork and many fees to meet and keep up with these requirements. We do not solicit donations in locations where we have not received written confirmation of compliance. To SEND DONATIONS or determine the status of compliance for any particular state visit http://www.gutenberg.org/fundraising/donate

While we cannot and do not solicit contributions from states where we have not met the solicitation requirements, we know of no prohibition against accepting unsolicited donations from donors in such states who approach us with offers to donate.

International donations are gratefully accepted, but we cannot make any statements concerning tax treatment of donations received from outside the United States. U.S. laws alone swamp our small staff.

Please check the Project Gutenberg Web pages for current donation methods and addresses. Donations are accepted in a number of other ways including checks, online payments and credit card donations. To donate, please visit: http://www.gutenberg.org/fundraising/donate

Section 5. General Information About Project Gutenberg-tm electronic works.

Professor Michael S. Hart is the originator of the Project Gutenberg-tm concept of a library of electronic works that could be freely shared with anyone. For thirty years, he produced and distributed Project Gutenberg-tm eBooks with only a loose network of volunteer support.

Project Gutenberg-tm eBooks are often created from several printed editions, all of which are confirmed as Public Domain in the U.S. unless a copyright notice is included. Thus, we do not necessarily keep eBooks in compliance with any particular paper edition.

Most people start at our Web site which has the main PG search facility:

http://www.gutenberg.org

This Web site includes information about Project Gutenberg-tm, including how to make donations to the Project Gutenberg Literary Archive Foundation, how to help produce our new eBooks, and how to subscribe to our email newsletter to hear about new eBooks.

Alaska Days with John Muir, by Samual Hall

A free ebook from http://manybooks.net/